D1272156

PARK SYNAGOGUE
CLEVELAND, OHIO
PRESENTED BY
IN HONOR OF
KRAVITZ MEMORIAL LIBRARY

PHOTOGRAPH BY ALAN W. RICHARDS

Princeton 1958

Martin Buber

JEWISH EXISTENTIALIST

By Malcolm L. Diamond

NEW YORK
Oxford University Press 1960

Library of Congress Catalogue Card Number: 60-7059

PRINTED IN THE UNITED STATES OF AMERICA

TO BARBARA

Preface

It is a tribute to the power of Martin Buber, a thoroughly religious thinker, that he should be one of the leading intellectual figures of our secular age. In fact, as his thought exerts an ever-increasing influence over a wide range of subjects, which vary from psychology to literary criticism and from political science to education, he is changing the meaning of the word "religion" itself. He knows of no authentic expression of religion that can be confined to the restricted domain of "spiritual" affairs; authentic religion involves man's genuine response to the whole of reality and this is the response of an I to a Thou.

The broad dissemination of Buber's outlook represents a gain for our culture, but it leads to misinterpretations of his thought. Some readers may be misled by secular thinkers who use Buber's insights while ignoring their religious matrix. Other readers may be misled by Christian commentators who overlook the distinctively Jewish character of that religious matrix.

Buber is a sophisticated thinker who is at home with the cultural developments of the avant-garde, but his talk of God as "the eternal Thou" should not be interpreted in a way that converts the term into a fashionable intellectual symbol divorced from the living God of our religious heritage. His thinking is deeply rooted in the ancient tradition of Judaism and he has found great inspiration in the teachings of Hasidism, a Jewish sect whose members, even today, resolutely insulate themselves against all facets of modern culture.

Buber is a passionate partisan of the Jewish Faith but he has been open to the word of God wherever it is manifest, and he has devoted intensive study to other great religious traditions, especially Christianity. His writings on the relation between Judaism and the Christian Faith which stemmed from it, are enormously significant contributions to the developing dialogue between adherents of these traditions. He regards Jesus as a religious teacher whose fundamentally Jewish outlook was radically altered by the teachings of Paul and of the early Church. But in his fervent expressions of admiration for Jesus as in his criticisms of Pauline Christianity, Buber remains a Jew who seeks to witness to the God of all religions.

Buber's religious witness has been expressed in a language whose great passion has misled some readers into supposing that he speaks of the mystical ecstacies of a religious élite, whereas no philosopher has been more concerned with the concrete character of everyday existence.

By developing the intimate link between Buber's philosophy and his interpretations of the major teachings of the Jewish tradition, I hope to clear up some of the misunderstandings of his work and shed light on the greatness of his contributions to modern life and thought.

Until the spring of 1958 I knew Martin Buber only as an intellectual figure. I had been deeply stirred by his outlook but the impact lacked the peculiar warmth that direct contact may engender. The three months he spent at Princeton University were a revelation. Not only did he live up to the image that he projects in his work, but his unfailing humor and his fresh approach to all experience surpassed all possible anticipation. He was curious about every detail of American culture from the complexities of its religious manifestations to the working of its supermarkets.

I can only hope that this study of Martin Buber, whose thought is of a piece with his life, reflects something of the wonder I felt at the man.

Malcolm L. Diamond

Princeton University
December 1959

Acknowledgments

This book naturally reflects the influence of my teachers, to all of whom I am grateful. I should especially like to mention the late David E. Roberts, who was Marcellus Hartley Professor of the Philosophy of Religion at Union Theological Seminary, and Professor Horace L. Friess of the Department of Philosophy, Columbia University.

Professor Louis I. Mink of the Department of Philosophy, Wesleyan College, provided invaluable assistance with his careful reading of the manuscript and the hours he spent in discussing it with me. Professor Paul Ramsey, my colleague in the Department of Religion, Princeton University, read the manuscript in various stages of its development and our many discussions of the work have been a fruitful source of stimulation and insight.

Professor James Ross of Drew University was very helpful in reading and criticizing the fourth chapter.

Mrs. Betty B. Bredemeier was most generous in giving me the benefit of her extensive editorial experience and helped me greatly with problems of style.

The Arthur J. Scribner Preceptorship, administered by Princeton University, provided me with a year's leave of absence during which this work was completed.

To Dr. Maurice S. Friedman of Sarah Lawrence College—whose work of interpreting, translating, and editing Buber's writings for the English-speaking world has put us all in his debt—I am indebted in a very special sense. His penetrating criticisms of my earlier approach to the work of Martin Buber have helped me to formulate a fresh approach for this volume.

Contents

Martin Buber: JEWISH EXISTENTIALIST

1. Introduction

IN 1958, at a public celebration in honor of his eightieth birthday, Martin Buber told the audience of his reluctance to talk about himself. He did so with a twinkle in his eyes — for he knew that we had gathered to hear him do just that — but all the same, he gave us an important clue to the power of his thought. He has talked intensely about his own experiences, yet in doing so he has displayed the reticence of the great poets who have not celebrated their experiencing selves but who have opened our hearts to the wonder of the world.

Although Buber's writing is at times rhapsodic, he is not a poet but a thinker — one of the leading religious thinkers of our age. Ironically, Buber is neither an academic philosopher nor is he a professional theologian. He readily admits that he must use the language of these disciplines to convey his ideas, but his freedom from the narrower concerns of professional guilds enables him to speak in a way that is both fresh and fertile. This does not mean that Buber is anti-philosophical or that he in any way lacks a grasp of the history of philosophy or theology. He is perfectly willing to discuss the points at which his outlook diverges from and approaches the leading figures of Western thought, but his interest is not directed toward philosophical or theological problems as such. He is more interested in the everyday encounters of man with the world.

Buber's difference from other thinkers is not absolute. All

philosophers and theologians deal with experience, otherwise their thought lacks vitality, but the difference of nuance is important. The reader who misses the sense in which professional considerations sit lightly on Buber, misses a central source of his power.

The most instructive way to observe the difference is to watch Buber among groups of philosophers or theologians. In such meetings he is bombarded with questions that are designed to elicit clear-cut answers that will enable the questioner to pigeonhole him. For example, he is often asked whether he really thinks that a man can encounter a tree as a partner in an I-Thou relation; the questioner hopes thereby to ascertain whether Buber is a panpsychist, that is, whether he holds the view that elements of consciousness permeate all things human and sub-human. Buber's answers are invariably frustrating, for he is not concerned about posing for a doctrinal picture. Instead, he turns the question back and asks his interlocutor to search his own life to see whether he can recall any experience in which a facet of nature arrested and engrossed him by the power of its uniqueness. Then and only then can Buber and his questioner talk, and necessarily in philosophical terms, of what transpired and of its significance for human existence. By contrast, the professional philosopher generally begins with an exposition of theoretical positions that might be taken in answer to the question, and turns to experience only to illustrate the aptness of one of the theories.

Buber's peculiar vitality as a person and a thinker stems, in large measure, from the fact that he has lived the life of the twentieth century to the fullest measure, bringing to his experience of its aspirations and agonies the heightened intensity so characteristic of the Jew. His thought, whose background we shall now consider, reveals an extraordinarily fruitful interaction between his involvement with Jewish loyalties and teachings and with European, especially German, culture.

His youth was spent in a predominantly Jewish area of Poland, where, until he was fourteen, he lived in the home of his grandfather, Salomon Buber, an outstanding scholar of the Haskalah, the Jewish Enlightenment. In the second half of the nineteenth century this movement effected a revolution in the life of East-European Jewry by adopting a modern approach to Jewish life and teachings, which, until that time, had been dominated by a medieval cast of mind. Salomon Buber's great contribution to Jewish scholarship was his preparation of definitive editions of many important texts. This combination of modern scholarship directed toward traditional Jewish texts prefigured one significant aspect of his grandson's career.

When Buber left this home to study at a secular secondary school in Lwow and later at the Universities of Vienna and Berlin, he lacked a thorough knowledge of the Jewish tradition. This was understandable since he was only in early adolescence — but he had mastered Hebrew and had become deeply attached to Jewish life and prayer. Despite this attachment he, like so many students both before and after his time, became estranged from Judaism as a result of an exposure to European culture, which was in a highly active state at that time. The intellectual currents that swirled around Buber at the turn of the century have been described in the first chapter of Hans Kohn's absorbing account of Buber's work and times. This book, unfortunately, has not been translated from the German.[1]

The main influence on Buber and his contemporaries was

the work of Nietzsche (1844–1900), who had challenged Western man to face up to the shallow, constricting, and hypocritical character of his traditional values and called upon him to transcend them by affirming life and its elemental forces. It was under the influence of this challenge that Buber, in one of his earliest public statements, speaking for his generation, declared: "We do not will a revolution, we are a revolution." [2]

Many schools of social thinking emerged in response to Nietzsche's revolutionary influence. Most of them involved little more than romantic posturing. But the social thought of Gustave Landauer (1869–1919), Buber's close friend, captured the sense of tension involved in Nietzsche's outlook. One of the tensions emphasized by Landauer had an enduring influence upon Buber. This was the tension between the highly centralized political state which tends to lose sight of the individual, and the smaller associations within the state that try to achieve genuine community.

Nietzsche influenced Buber's style both directly, through the example of works such as his *Thus Spake Zarathustra,* and indirectly, through his influence on the late romantics with whom Buber had much in common. He shared their tendency to emotive expression and their passionate involvement with art. His writings contain many illustrations drawn from the arts, and early in his career he wrote a number of essays on painting, the drama, and literature.

The revival of Kantian thinking, especially as exemplified in the work of Hermann Cohen (1842–1918), brought Buber into intimate relation with the main line of the German philosophical tradition. However, as we have already remarked, Buber has never been interested in philosophical problems as such. He was influenced to develop the absorption with concrete social and cultural concerns that is so characteristic of his thought by the example of his teachers — Georg Simmel (1858–1918), whose philosophy was sociologically oriented, and Wilhelm Dilthey (1833–1911), who spent a lifetime creating a philosophy of culture.

As a student Buber was enthralled by the mystical teachings of many religious traditions, and his doctoral dissertation was a study of the thought of a number of Christian mystics of the Renaissance and the Reformation. One reason for Buber's attraction to mystical teachings was their emphasis upon the rare moments of ecstasy. Ecstatic experiences pointed the way to the concentration of life energies and through it to the outpouring of creative vitality that he found so appealing a part of Nietzsche's message. Therefore, Buber's early writings, written while he was still under the influence of Nietzsche, express the mystical passion for unity. Buber sought for that ecstatic unity within the soul of man that enables the mystic to approach the world with renewed power. Ultimately the mystic seeks to unite with the absolute — that true reality whose being and power is the ground of the world of everyday experience, which the mystics depreciate as illusory.

Buber actually achieved a concentration of his creative powers early in life and his remarkable gifts as a writer and lecturer won him a great deal of attention when he was still a very young man. Yet this early success left him dissatisfied with his life, because he was oppressed by a sense of rootlessness. This, he has assured us, was not unusual in young intellectuals; but it was intensified in Jews who had broken with their tradition without having the stabilizing factor of an organic relation to a native soil and culture.[3]

His search for roots led Buber to his earliest form of

Jewish affirmation—active participation in the Zionist movement, then in its infancy. He soon found himself opposing the political Zionism of the dominant group, which was primarily interested in establishing a Jewish State in order to protect the Jewish people from the ravages of anti-Semitism. He emerged as a leading spokesman of a faction that regarded the founding of a political state as only one phase of a Jewish Renaissance. This faction was more concerned with cultural creativity than with personal security and they hoped to achieve integration within European culture by achieving wholeness in their lives as Jews. This wholeness had been impossible through the many centuries of the Diaspora (the dispersion of the Jews throughout the nations of the world), because legislation forbidding Jews to own land had prevented them from having an intimate relation to the soil. Buber's Zionism was characterized by a passion for correcting the imbalance in Jewish life—with its excessive emphasis on intellectual, commercial, and professional pursuits—which had been the result of this exclusion from agriculture.

Even this active role in the Zionist cause left Buber dissatisfied with the quality of his life, because, as he was later to write: "I professed Judaism before I really knew it."[4] In order to come to know it, he turned to an intensive study of Jewish sources and came upon the teachings of Hasidism, which crucially influenced his development.

The name Hasidism derives from the Hebrew word *Hasid*, generally translated as "a pious one." The movement was founded in the villages of Poland in the middle of the eighteenth century by Israel ben Eliezer (1700–1760), called the Baal Shem Tov, which literally means "Master of the Good Name" (the name of God), and spread through Eastern

Europe among Jews who were living according to the thought and folkways of their fathers. In the midst of the upheavals of one hundred and fifty years of history, its adherents doggedly resisted all change and entered the twentieth century as determined to preserve their medieval customs and outlook as they were bound to preserve their allegiance to the God of Israel. Since they persist as a sect within Judaism to this day, with important communities in Israel, the United States, and England, one can observe them and see that their efforts have been successful in both respects.

As a boy, Buber had seen Hasidic life in the villages near his home. Although these groups represented a marked decline from those that existed in the period of greatness initiated by the Baal Shem Tov, Buber was able to form impressions of the creative communal spirit that once characterized their life. His discovery of Hasidic teachings in the early years of this century therefore provided a potent link to his childhood as well as to the Jewish tradition. The attraction of the movement was so strong that, in 1904, he withdrew from his active life of writing and lecturing and devoted five years of intensive study to Hasidic teachings. This study convinced him that its early phase, dating roughly from 1750 to 1825, had produced a surge of creative religious living that was unparalleled in history — because it was not confined to withdrawn monastic communities of the "religious" but was manifest in ordinary Jewish villages among all sorts of people.

Buber's encounter with Hasidism, which emphasized joyful worship of God in the here and now of this world and this life, transformed him from a European intellectual, groping for Jewish roots, into a thinker whose cast of mind and deepest loyalties were indelibly Jewish. His characterization of the prophets of Israel as "national-universalists" applies equally to him.[5] His passionate concern for humanity is rooted in the particularity of his loyalty to his people and their faith.

When Buber emerged from his intensive study of Hasidic teachings, he was confronted by a fresh source of intellectual stimulation. During the first decade of this century the writings of Soren Kierkegaard (1813–1855) had been translated from Danish into German. The fact that the work of this Christian thinker became available in what was certainly, at that time, the most important language of Western philosophy, triggered the development of existentialism as a major philosophy of our age. Kierkegaard insisted that philosophical inquiry be concentrated on the total existence — body and mind, will and emotions — of the individual. A system which was not relevant to the concrete concerns of the individual could, at best, be only a project for thought that told us nothing about existence. Kierkegaard claimed that the speculative system of Hegelian idealism, which was the dominant philosophy of his day, was not only irrelevant to the lives of ordinary men, it was irrelevant to the lives of the philosophers themselves. Even the philosophers are existing individuals, and he also claimed that the concrete person had no place in the Hegelian system.

There was a great difference between Kierkegaard's rejection of philosophical idealism and that of Nietzsche, which had exerted such a strong influence on Buber's early writings. Kierkegaard opposed philosophical rationalism from the standpoint of religious faith, whereas Nietzsche had opposed it from the standpoint of a human creativity that would replace the God whose death he proclaimed. As Buber responded to Hasidism and other Jewish teachings, he moved increasingly toward a personal affirmation of Jewish faith; for this reason, Kierkegaard's religious outlook became increasingly relevant to his thought. It exerted a powerful effect on Buber's existential understanding of truth and upon his view of the way in which contemporary men may relate themselves creatively to the message of the Bible.

Although Buber never lost his great admiration for Kierkegaard, he became one of Kierkegaard's severest critics. The Pauline Christianity manifest in Kierkegaard's writings was highly individualistic in its approach to religion, and pessimistic about man. This stood in contrast to the more optimistic Jewish tradition which influenced Buber. Even at the points of his maximum indebtedness to him, Buber filtered Kierkegaard's existentialism through the teachings of Hasidism. However, the reaction was not all in one direction. Reading Kierkegaard led Buber to shift his interest from the mystical aspect of Hasidic teaching, with its emphasis on the rare moments of ecstatic worship, to the side of its teachings that emphasized infusing the routines of everyday life with the breath of eternity.

This shift is reflected in the development of Buber's philosophy. As he became more existential he became increasingly disenchanted with mysticism. He came to regard its claim to union with the absolute as an illusion, since the separated self persists. He came to see its very preoccupation with unity as one which failed to value the multiplicity of existence. Furthermore, he found that the mystical emphasis on the rare moments of religious exaltation tore religion out of the fabric of the everyday life of man. In his greatest work, *I and Thou,* which was published in German in 1923, he sharply criticized the mystical emphasis on unity, and spoke instead of relation — relation as most fully manifest in love between man and wife — as the central clue to the meaning of existence.[6]

Buber's thought was given definitive expression in *I and Thou.* He has never altered the fundamental position he elaborated in that book. His subsequent work has involved a clarification of it as well as its application to a wide number of areas, many of which relate to Jewish subjects.

From the time of his contact with Hasidic teachings, Buber has been involved with Jewish life and thought. In 1916, he became the editor of *Der Jude,* a periodical to which he contributed many articles promulgating the Zionist views that led him to break with the purely political wing of the movement. By 1924, when he relinquished his post as editor, the periodical had become one of the foremost expressions of serious Jewish thinking in Germany.

In 1923, Buber accepted an appointment to the newly created chair of Jewish philosophy at the University of Frankfurt. At that time there was a revival of Jewish studies taking place in Germany. The Jewish theologian Franz Rosenzweig (1886–1929) took the lead in establishing a unique experiment in adult Jewish education in Frankfurt, and Buber played a vital role in the work. It was an attempt to introduce a generation that had been estranged from its heritage to the key texts of the Jewish tradition. Since learning Hebrew and Aramaic was out of the question for most students, they worked with translations. Out of the need to provide a German text of the Old Testament that would reflect the thought, structure, and rhythm of the original Hebrew, the Rosenzweig-Buber translation was launched.

This was probably the first time in the history of Old

Testament translation that fidelity to Hebrew, rather than to the language into which it was being set, was made the primary aim. For example, although the Semitic original delights in a form of word play that involves considerable repetition of words and phrases, all other translations follow Western esthetic principles and avoid undue repetition. Rosenzweig and Buber preserved the word play of the original, even where they had to construct new forms of German words in order to do it.

At Rosenzweig's death, the work had been carried as far as the book of Isaiah (in the Hebrew order of the texts), and Buber has continued the work alone, having recently, in 1958, completed his translation of the Psalms. But of even greater significance than his work of translation are his many volumes of biblical interpretation; they have established him as one of the leading commentators of our time.

Buber's chair in Jewish philosophy at the University of Frankfurt was later expanded to embrace the history of religions, a discipline which had long been one of his major interests. In 1933, when the Nazis came to power, this phase of his career came to an end. From that time, until he went to Israel in 1938 to assume the chair in social philosophy at Hebrew University, he was a source of inspiration to the German-Jewish community in the midst of its anguish; he taught in Jewish schools, lectured, wrote, and above all, he provided the example of a courage that was rooted in Jewish faith.[7]

As a result of the stimulus provided by the creative communal experiments in Israel and in response to the need to focus his thinking along the lines dictated by his position as professor of social philosophy, Buber wrote *Paths in*

Utopia, a history of socialistic thinking and a statement of his own position.[8] This book represents the fruits of almost fifty years of study and reflection in the area. Living in Israel also stimulated him to his most sustained expression of Zionist convictions, *Israel and Palestine;* in it the attitude of the Jewish people to the soil of Palestine is traced historically from its biblical expressions on through modern Zionism.[9]

Since he retired from the Hebrew University in 1951, Buber has been extraordinarily active as author and lecturer. In this latter capacity, his travels all over the world have enabled him to witness, indeed to accelerate, the amazing increase in his influence. He has, in fact, lived to see his thought become a part of the intellectual currency of our age.

2. I and Thou

THE outlook expressed in Martin Buber's *I and Thou* can affect all phases of intellectual life, because it is a way of apprehending and deepening every form of experience. It is a philosophy, indeed it is called "the philosophy of dialogue," but it directs itself toward what Buber terms real questions rather than toward philosophical problems. For Buber, philosophical problems emerge only when men reflect upon the real questions, that is, on questions which engage the total person rather than the intellect alone, and questions that involve important issues. For example, a young Hasid approached his master in tears saying, "I am after all alive in this world, a being created with all the senses and all the limbs, but I do not know what it is I was created for and what I am good for in this world." [1]

Real questions arise out of a man's self-awareness. They cannot be answered conclusively; yet asking them is a necessary part of being human and reflecting on them is a major function of philosophy. While it is a function of philosophy to reflect upon these questions, the further its language and mode of thinking move from the experiences that engender them, the more inadequate its treatment will be. Questions concerning the nature and destiny of man cannot be properly considered apart from concrete situations. Relevance to life-experience is a cardinal point of Buber's philosophy.

Buber is not alone among contemporary philosophers in emphasizing life-relevance as the starting and finishing point of philosophy. But the term may have many meanings. The pragmatists understand it in terms of the capacity of scientific intelligence to cope with problems relating to the social concerns of man. But in his understanding of life-relevance, and of so many issues, Buber shares the perspectives of that disparate group of philosophical individualists who somehow manage to strike enough chords in common to evoke the descriptive term — existentialists.[2] The term is difficult to define, not only because of the individualism of existential thinkers but also because of the confusions deriving from its association with the work of Jean-Paul Sartre. Sartre is certainly a significant representative of atheistic existentialism, but any study of existentialism must include thinkers whose conclusions are radically opposed to his. We have already noted that the father of the movement was Soren Kierkegaard, a Christian thinker who, in the first half of the nineteenth century, launched a radical protest against philosophical rationalism. A central dictum of his approach was that even the highest degree of rational consistency in a philosophical system cannot coerce existence into conformity with its conclusions. Existence, as encountered by the man of flesh and bone is not an interplay of rational consistencies, but a panorama of possibilities encountered in a world of fact. The central task for the individual is to achieve authentic selfhood by means of resolute decisions. This summons to free and responsible decision is the stuff of existence and the focus of existentialism.

It is the stuff of other modes of philosophizing as well. Decision and freedom play a role in every system of philosophical ethics. And the primacy of actual experience over intellectual speculation, which is a major point of existentialism, has been the hall mark of the venerable tradition of empirical philosophy. But the empirical tradition has taken all the data of experience — of willing and thinking, sensing and feeling — and analyzed them in an attitude of detachment. This tradition, no less than the rational one it opposed, attempted to strip human judgments of subjective involvement and passion. By contrast, the existentialists have consciously adopted the posture of passionate engagement as an integral part of their philosophizing. Objective reason may be successful in coping with nature, but the existentialists insist that attempts to deal with what we have called "the real questions" from the standpoint of the detached observer can only lead to falsification and self-deception: to falsification, because the vital experiences out of which values such as freedom and justice are posited are eviscerated in the effort to strip them of their emotional thrust; to self-deception, because the "objective" observer of religious, political, and other phenomena of the same order, is personally engaged, whether he likes it or not, and can only preserve his objective stance by obscuring the nature of his involvement from himself.

This passionate approach to life's fundamental issues has hitherto been the province of literature, which is the reason that existential philosophies, even when couched in the most complex terminology, strike a somewhat literary note. They attempt to express the sensible overtones of concrete experience. It is, therefore, not always easy to discern the boundary between philosophical existentialism and literature. Students of existentialism often refer to literary figures such as Dostoyevsky and Kafka as existentialists, and the adjective "existential" has become a generally accepted way of referring to any expression of passionate concern with questions of man's destiny.

In the more restricted sense of the term, the existentialists are thinkers who participate in the philosophical tradition of the Western world, but find that its normal modes of discourse lend themselves all too readily to an objective approach to reality. By contrast, the existentialists convey a sense of direct involvement with questions of human destiny even when their language is strained and cumbersome. One need only compare the traditional philosophical expression, "the problem of immortality," with "being-toward-one's-death," a category drawn from the thought of one of the leading existentialists, to sense the difference in psychological immediacy and personal urgency.[3] This almost literary sense of immediacy does not set the existentialists utterly apart from the tradition of Western philosophy; there are existential elements in many of its key figures from Plato onward, but in the work of the existentialists these elements are central.

The common concerns of the existentialists arise out of their effort to affirm truth from the standpoint of engagement. They focus on the great themes of life and on the drama of history. They tend to ignore such technical areas of philosophy as logic and the theory of knowledge.

The majority of them, religious and atheistic alike, take a dark view of "man's predicament." They summon the individual to an authentic life, but they emphasize the barriers to its realization to the extent that they seem to encourage neurotic preoccupation with the agonies of existence. They extoll freedom, but they do so by emphasizing the anxieties and anguish of the decisions involved in giving it authentic expression. It was not without justification that Marjorie Grene called her study of the existentialists *Dreadful Freedom*.[4]

In *I and Thou* Buber's affinities with existentialism are obvious. In addition to its literary tone, its approach to meaning is one of passionate engagement. But his thought has interacted intimately with the world-affirming tradition of Judaism, which has always cautioned its adherents against overanxious preoccupation with sin, so that it stands in sharp contrast to the anguished emphasis of most existentialists. Compared to their views, Buber's outlook, which might seem pessimistic from the standpoint of rationalism, is quite optimistic. For this reason, his work is often omitted from studies of existentialism, which have tended to stress its grim features.

Some otherwise astute interpreters of Buber's thought have contributed to the confusion concerning his relation to existentialism by speaking of an earlier, relatively unimportant, phase of his work as "existential," while reserving the terms "dialogical thinking" or "the philosophy of dialogue" for the mature and final stage of his thought inaugurated by *I and Thou*.[5] These are appropriate names for the philosophy expressed in that work. They suggest the give and take of genuine conversation between men in existential confrontation, and they point to the possibility of genuine relatedness between man and the world. But the dialogical thinking of Buber's later writings is as existential as that of the earlier stage upon which these interpreters bestowed the term "existential." *I and Thou* and his subsequent philosophical works are simply a more felicitous form of existential expression, because in them, his existential perspective is enriched by a more profound appreciation of the Jewish tradition. In fact, the fusion of existential thinking with the world-affirming spirit of Judaism is Martin Buber's great contribution to contemporary intellectual life.

I and Thou begins with the declaration: "To man the world is twofold, in accordance with his twofold attitude." [6] The two attitudes that man can direct toward the world must not be taken merely psychologically. What is indicated by the term "attitude" is a fundamental posture, a way of setting the self toward the world and any of the beings one meets within it. Buber calls these fundamental postures the I-Thou and the I-It. The terms are striking but highly artificial, especially in English, which does not indulge the philosopher's inclination to create his own vocabulary as does the German in which the work was written. At the outset readers may be puzzled by these key terms. They cannot be understood in themselves; their meaning can only become clear in the context of the book.

The terms I-It and I-Thou stand, respectively, in intimate relation to the existential distinction between the detached approach to truth and that of engagement, but we must remember that Buber's thought bears his own peculiar stamp. His illustrations provide the only reliable guide to his meaning.

A common source of misunderstandings are the correlations which Buber's philosophically sophisticated readers are tempted to draw between his thought and that of leading figures in the Western tradition. For example, the reader familiar with the Kantian dictum that a man ought never to be treated only as a means but always as an end in himself, may conclude that the I-It posture is one which an "I" ought to assume toward things, toward an "It," whereas the I-Thou posture is appropriate to a description of relations between persons.[7] But the perspective of *I and Thou* cuts across this familiar distinction. It is true that the terms derive from attitudes more commonly held between man and things on the one hand, and between man and man on the other, but it is a basic aspect of Buber's outlook that both attitudes are manifested in man's relation to any and all beings.

The attitude of detachment, the I-It, is often adopted by the scientific investigator, and he can hold it in relation to man as well as in relation to things. Indeed, the effort to attain objective insight into men through an attitude of detachment is the basic drive of the social sciences.

As both postures may be directed to all beings, to things as well as to persons, so too, both postures may be held by all manner of men regardless of their vocations. For example, another common distinction which loses some of its usual connotations within the framework of *I and Thou* is that between the scientist and the artist. Although most people readily concede that the social scientist attempts to approach men in an attitude of detachment, they usually think of the novelist as being passionately engaged with his subject matter. From the standpoint of the philosophy of dialogue, both, insofar as they approach men as a source of data, exemplify the I-It attitude. For the two postures are not rigid compartments into which various types of people permanently fit — the scientist into the I-It, the artist into the I-Thou — they are modes of personal existence that appear alternately in all men. "There are not two kinds of man, but two poles of humanity." [8]

The "I" of the I-It differs fundamentally from the "I" of the I-Thou; in the I-It posture the "I" holds back —

measuring, using, and even seeking to control the object of its attention—but never, as in the I-Thou relation, affirming the other just as it is in itself.

Since it is clear that the I-Thou posture is the one to which the deeper meaning of existence is disclosed, readers are sometimes misled into thinking that the I-It is a negative, or even an evil, category in Buber's thought. This is far from being the case, ". . . human life neither can nor ought to overcome the connection with It. . . ."[9] The relation is necessary and appropriate to many activities. Through knowledge acquired in detachment, man is able to achieve a reliable perspective on the world and a considerable degree of control over nature. It is in the It perspective that physicists all over the world can communicate by means of mathematical symbols that are free of the cultural nuances that haunt words such as "democracy" and "freedom" and make them susceptible to so many radically conflicting interpretations.

The I-It posture is not evil any more than power or any other basic element of existence is in itself evil. Power becomes evil when it is abused. Buber cites Napoleon as an instance of a demonic leader, because he drew men to himself by convincing them that he was concerned with them as persons when in reality he had no genuine involvement with them.[10] In the realm of thought, the It posture becomes evil when it oversteps its limits and claims to encompass the totality of truth, thereby choking off the possibility of response to the deeper levels of meaning that may emerge from I-Thou encounters.

The I-It attitude becomes a source of evil whenever the individual becomes so addicted to it that he remains absorbed in his own purposes and concerns when he should be responding in a fresh way to the beings he meets. "The subjective knowledge of the one turning-towards about his turning-towards, this holding back of an I which does not enter into the action with the rest of the person, an I to which the action is an object — all this dispossesses the moment, takes away its spontaneity." [11]

While certain that the I-It attitude is not evil, that indeed, ". . . without It man cannot live," Buber warns that, "he who lives with It alone is not a man." [12]

Just as all beings may be regarded as objects by a self that assumes the I-It posture of detachment, so too all beings may serve as a partner to man in the I-Thou encounter. However, Buber divides them into three spheres of relation: encounters between man and nature; between man and man; and between man and "spiritual beings," a term that unfortunately suggests extrasensory phenomena. As Buber uses it, the term refers to all the products of human creativity — to works of art, philosophical systems, and the like.

What Buber means by the I-Thou encounter cannot be explained, it can only be indicated. The author of the first significant study of Buber to appear in English, Jacob B. Agus, made this point when he said that, if we are to understand the uniqueness of the I-Thou relation, we must heed Buber's appeal to find an echo of his words in our own life.[13] But Dr. Agus himself ignored this insight and proceeded to describe the relation with a host of abstract terms such as presentness, centrality, and exclusiveness. This set a precedent which all too many subsequent studies have followed. I should like to depart from it by describing two personal experiences and showing how the language and outlook of *I and Thou* sheds light upon them. Since these were experiences with works of art, they may serve to illustrate the third sphere of encounter, the relation between man and "spiritual beings."

For many weeks I had looked forward to hearing a performance of Beethoven's Fourth Piano Concerto, not only because it was one of my favorite works, but because Clifford Curzon and George Szell, who were to perform it, had, in my experience, consistently maintained the crucial tension between soloist and orchestra. As it turned out, the performance was bitterly disappointing.

> *The Thou meets me through grace — it is not found by seeking.*[14]

One cannot plan to experience an I-Thou encounter any more than one can plan to fall in love. Yet without seeking, which in this case involved putting myself in the way of the music, there is no possibility of an I-Thou encounter taking place.

The peculiar combination of planning and spontaneity that stands at the heart of the I-Thou encounter may be illustrated by means of another experience. In this instance I went to hear Bruno Walter conduct a performance of Beethoven's Seventh Sympany, but only because I was urged to go by friends. I myself regard Walter's interpretations of Beethoven as too romantic.

On this occasion, grace was present. The first few bars challenged all preconceptions. The pastoral first movement was succeeded by the somber dread and sobbing passion of the second, and the effect was enhanced by the sight of Walter leading one section of the orchestra after the other into the theme until they united in a chorus of almost unbearable anguish. This incredible intensity was maintained throughout the symphony — a performance worthy of the music.

> *The Thou meets me. But I step into direct relation with it. Hence the relation means being chosen and choosing, suffering and action in one. . . .*[15]

During the Curzon-Szell performance, my attention wandered; I recalled other performances of the work and compared them with it, and I anticipated the reactions of companions and critics. In the performance of the Seventh Symphony, that performance, and it alone, was present.

> *Every real relation with a being or life in the world is exclusive. Its Thou is freed, steps forth, is single, and confronts you.*[16]

In the encounter the sense of objective space and time dissolved. I was not aware of being in Carnegie Hall in New York City, nor of the minutes that elapsed in the course of the performance.

> *The world of It is set in the context of space and time. The world of Thou is not set in the context of either of these.*[17]

There is a time that marks the encounter, but it is not chronological time, whose present is a contentless instant between past and future, it is the filled time of the duration of the encounter itself.

> *It is your present; only while you have it do you have the present.*[18]

To attempt, during the performance itself, to account for its greatness in terms of cause and effect, of esthetic principles and criteria, would dissolve the spontaneity and destroy the presence.

> *So long as the heaven of Thou is spread out over me the winds of causality cower at my heels. . . .*[19]

Listening to previous performances of Walter's Beethoven, I had been aware of an opposition within myself. At times the emotions had been stirred, but the intellect had warned that they were being taken in. In this performance, the entire self responded; the intelligence was at one with the tears.

> *The primary word I-Thou can only be spoken with the whole being.*[20]

While the whole being must encounter the Thou as exclusively present, there is no ecstatic union involved, no mystical fusing of the self with the "larger whole."

> [*The Thou*] *. . . teaches you to meet others and to hold your ground when you meet them.*[21]

Should I, in the midst of the encounter, become conscious of listening, conscious of enjoying a great "experience," my Thou vanishes on the spot, and I find myself in the domain of It, preparing comments on the sublimity of the performance.

> *As soon as the relation has been worked out or has been permeated with a means, the Thou becomes an object among objects — perhaps the chief, but still one of them, fixed in its size and its limits.*[22]

Yet performances end, relations are disrupted, and the intense concentration of the momentary encounters cannot endure. In order to get on with our living we must step back from absorption with the Thou.

But this is the exalted melancholy of our fate, that every Thou in our world must become an It.[23]

All facets of human creativity are encompassed in the sphere of the spirit — from the tools and carvings of primitive man through the greatest works of art produced by advanced cultures — from the savage strife of the great epics to the most rarefied systems of philosophy and mathematics. But it is the relation between man and man, the human sphere of encounter, which provides the obvious example of the I-Thou relation and suggests the term "Thou." Here the partner is articulate and the relation is characterized by mutuality of understanding and speech. Persons may say "Thou" to one another, but it is not the mouthing of the word that is crucial. The crucial factor is the fact that the self is engaged by an other, who here, as in the other two spheres of the I-Thou relation, stands over against the self as a concrete individual. The German word *gegenüber* is awkwardly translated by the phrase "over against," but the use of this phrase is important since it suggests the sense in which Buber's dialogical thinking opposes the mystical emphasis upon the ecstatic "union" of the self and the other.

The I-Thou relation is most fully realized in love between man and wife. Here arises what Buber calls the exemplary bond, two people revealing the Thou to each other. Love involves the recognition and confirmation of the other in his or her uniqueness, and to this end, marriage affords the greatest length of time and the greatest degree of intimacy.

Although Buber is sometimes accused of romanticism, his view of love is set in conscious opposition to the romantic understanding of love as feeling. The romantic view is so prevalent today that it has become the greatest problem of contemporary marriage, for it leads people to believe that when the romantic feeling ceases, responsibility toward the other ceases, and one must seek fulfillment by finding a new partner who will awaken the "sincere" feeling of love. But love is not a feeling, "Love is responsibility of an I for a Thou." [24] Feelings are important to marriage, but they are not its essence. Marriage develops its own rhythm and involves withdrawal and self-disclosure, disruption and reconciliation. The heart of marriage, as of love, is in responding to the other within a framework created by the relationship itself.[25]

> Feelings dwell in man; but man dwells in his love. That is no metaphor, but the actual truth. Love does not cling to the I in such a way as to have the Thou only for its "content," its object; but love is *between* I and Thou. The man who does not know this, with his very being know this, does not know love; even though he ascribes to it the feelings he lives through, experiences, enjoys, and expresses.[26]

Love cannot be genuine without being grounded in the I-Thou relation, but the relation is not to be equated with love. In fact, ". . . the man who straightforwardly hates is nearer to relation than the man without hate and love." [27] This is important because contemporary life encourages the indifference that precludes, as hate does not, all possibility of recognizing the other as a man like oneself. A man expressing irritation with an elevator operator must turn toward him. He may then recognize his humanity. The man who enters the cubicle and does nothing but mutter a number with the same indifference with which he would press a button in an automatic elevator, can come to no such realization.

Readers often imagine, perhaps in response to Buber's poetic language, that the I-Thou encounters are highly specialized affairs comparable to mystical ecstasy. This is emphatically not the case. Buber does not attempt to point to mysteries that can only be discerned by an elite. "The life of dialogue is no privilege of intellectual activity like dialectic. It does not begin in the upper story of humanity. It begins no higher than where humanity begins. There are no gifted and ungifted here, only those who give themselves and those who withhold themselves."[28] Neither is the life of dialogue to be understood as an activity reserved for special occasions that are removed from the routines of everyday life. "You put before me [as one whose routine precludes the possibility of the I-Thou relation] the man taken up with duty and business. Yes precisely him I mean, him in the factory, in the shop, in the office, in the mine, on the tractor, at the printing press. . . . Dialogue is not an affair of spiritual luxury. . . ."[29]

No special intuitions are necessary to the consummation of an I-Thou relation, and no beings, however mundane, are excluded from its scope. Buber has even written of an encounter with a mineral fragment.[30] This observation may introduce the sphere of encounter with the realm of nature, embracing the inanimate world (from the stones to the stars) and the living world (from patches of moss through the animal kingdom). It also brings us to Buber's often challenged account of his encounter with a tree.

He begins by enumerating a number of perspectives from

which a tree may be considered: botanical type, chemical composition, physical structure, material for a painting. Then he adds: "It can, however, also come about, if I have both will and grace, that in considering the tree I become bound up in relation to it. The tree is now no longer It. I have been seized by the power of exclusiveness." [31]

Since the term I-Thou so strongly suggests the personal, critics often seem to believe that Buber imagines that the tree is aware of him in the same sense that he is aware of it. They do so, however, in the face of his denial of any such notion. "The tree will have a consciousness, then, similar to our own? Of that I have no experience." What is of central significance for Buber is our ability to affirm the tree as existing just as it is, in its own right, independently of our purposes. "The tree is no impression, no play of my imagination, no value depending on my mood; but it is bodied over against me and has to do with me, as I with it — only in a different way." [32]

Buber certainly recognizes differences in encounters between man and nature and those between man and man. In fact, he refers to the human sphere as the main portal and to the other two spheres as side gates. When we wonder why, in the face of this, he persists in using a term as personal as "I-Thou" to describe relations between man and natural beings and man and works of art, we must simply weigh the differences against the similarities. We have already noted the latter; they relate to one's total posture. In the I-Thou mode, detachment is overcome; the other being is bodied over against one as an exclusive center of attention and affirmed independently of the purposes of the experiencing self.

Yet it would seem that Buber does not weigh the differences heavily enough. After describing the encounter with the tree he adds, "Let no attempt be made to sap the strength from the meaning of the relation: relation is mutual." [33] For as Buber readily admits, there can be no mutuality in the sense that a tree or a work of art can in any way be conscious of man! Whatever encounters Buber may have experienced, his talk of mutuality in man's relation with beings that lack consciousness introduces more confusion than illumination. Our mode of apprehending any and all beings does vary radically as between the It and the Thou postures, but mutuality is not one of the factors that constitutes the difference.

Buber himself is unclear on this point, almost conceding it in his admission that even between man and man a Thou relation may take place without full mutuality. "Even if the man to whom I say Thou is not aware of it in the midst of his experience, yet relation may exist." [34] In the "Postscript" to *I and Thou* which appeared in 1958, some thirty-five years after the first German edition, this hint is expanded by means of a number of illustrations of human relations: teacher-pupil, psychotherapist-patient, pastor-parishoner. In these relations full mutuality is impossible because of the very nature of the relationship; but Buber insists that the I-Thou encounter may, and indeed should, take place within them.[35]

In the same "Postscript" he refines his view of the sphere of nature by means of a distinction between the animal world which stands at the threshold of mutuality, and the inanimate world which stands below it. But even the inanimate is granted some form of expressiveness that points toward mutuality. Although Buber says that, "Our habits of thought make it difficult for us to see. . . ." just what this is.[36] The treatment of this theme as it pertains to the sphere of the spirit is no less vague.[37]

It is significant that categories such as exclusiveness, presentness, engagement, concreteness, and the rest did not have to be reworked in a postscript. Mutuality, in being so extensively refined, assumes a rather tortured character which shifts with each relation. It is present in full measure in some encounters within the human sphere and in a more limited way in others. But it can only be applied in the most tenuous way to the other two spheres. It would have been better if Buber had given up the notion that it is as applicable to a general description of the I-Thou encounter as are his other categories.

There are more pressing problems connected with the dialogical approach to reality than the problem of mutuality. The most critical of these is the problem of judgment. From the earliest epoch of philosophy, thinkers have attempted to establish an objective basis of judgment that would liberate philosophical, political, religious, and similar issues from the relativities of time and place and from the vagaries of personal opinion. Yet in the philosophy of dialogue, we find that it is only the realm of It whose ". . . organization can be surveyed and brought out again and again; gone over with closed eyes and verified with open eyes." [38] Within the realm of Thou — which embraces all the significant questions of human destiny — objective ascertaining and verifying of meaning is not possible. The attempt to do so forces one to step back into the detachment of the I-It posture, which is necessarily unfaithful to the meanings disclosed in the original encounter.

Buber's critics insist that, even if we accept his basic philosophical approach, his lack of an objective criterion for distinguishing between authentic and delusory I-Thou encounters prevents his forming valid judgments with regard to these great issues. They claim that his philosophy of dialogue must regard any point of view which appeals to the perspective of engagement as valid. One critic notes that since Hitler apparently experienced some form of an I-Thou encounter with the German people Buber has no criterion by which he can discriminate between this and any other instance of an I-Thou relation.[39]

Buber's answer is emphatic. There is and can be no objective criterion which will establish universal standards of judgment regarding the fundamental issues of human existence, because there are no philosophical arguments, grounded in logic and appealing to sense experience, which can coerce men into uniformity on these matters. The philosophers' search for the objective criterion of knowledge is as futile as was the alchemists' search for the touchstone that would transmute base metal into gold.

Buber employs criteria frequently, and his thought has more content than that of almost any other contemporary thinker, but neither the criteria nor the contents are objective. He values the I-Thou encounters between man and man more highly than those that take place between man and the beings in the other two spheres. His criterion is the greater degree of mutuality possible in human encounters. This criterion arises out of the richness of the encounters themselves. Buber could not demonstrate its validity to an esthete who places greater value on encounters with works of art.

Buber cannot demonstrate the validity of his criteria objectively, because, when we deal with the fundamental questions of human existence, we have no way of rising above the posture of engagement to a more valid perspective. This is the key to his existential approach to truth. Truth for Buber, as for all the existentialists, is more a matter of moral striving than of an intellectual solution of problems. "Human truth," he writes, "becomes real when one tries to translate one's relationship to truth into the reality of one's own life. And human truth can be communicated only if one throws one's self into the process and answers for it with one's self." [40]

Buber emphasizes the risk involved in becoming engaged in social, political, and religious questions when one can have no guarantee of the truth of one's position. He insists that all the trumpet blasts calling for a return to absolute standards of truth and falsity and right and wrong must prove futile. The absolutes which men erect in their midst — absolutes of scripture or church, thought or party — promise men security; but ultimately, they result in fanatical adherence to these absolutes as embodiments of *the* Truth, or in cynical disillusionment.

In contrast to the partisans of absolutism Buber writes that he has occasionally described his standpoint as a "narrow ridge." [41] One stands on this ridge when affirming the existence of the absolute as the ultimate ground of being and truth while refusing to grant absolute validity to any human expressions of this absolute. That is why Buber speaks of "human truth"; men may live truth authentically, but they cannot express it conclusively. I-Thou encounters disclose the meaning of existence, but they do not provide a perspective which can incorporate this meaning in objective form. The "narrow ridge" rises between views which hold that truth may be embodied in propositions that are objectively demonstrable and the various forms of relativism which deny the existence of the absolute altogether and reduce truth to matters of taste and to the status of subjective feelings.

> And if one still asks if one may be certain of finding what is right on this steep path, once again the answer is *No;* there is no certainty. There is only a chance; but there is no other. The risk does not insure the truth for us; but it, and it alone, leads us to where the breath of truth is to be felt.[42]

There are many who regard this existential approach to truth as a form of irrational rhetoric. But Buber is not an irrationalist; he does not set some non-rational faculty, such as intuition, above reason and use it as the path to truth. He regards reason as relevant to all human concerns and he uses reason to explore the limits of the I-It posture in relation to social, moral, and religious issues.

However, there is one respect in which Buber is vulnerable to the charge of irrationalism. He has failed to elaborate the sense in which detached knowledge, gained in the I-It attitude, may enrich the meaning conveyed within the I-Thou relation. But he has provided us with an important clue. In order to effect an I-Thou encounter with a tree it is not necessary, he says, ". . . for me to give up any of the ways in which I consider the tree. There is nothing from which I would have to turn my eyes away in order to see, and no knowledge that I would have to forget. Rather is everything, [every kind of I-It knowledge of the tree] picture and movement, species and type, law and number, indivisibly united in this event."[43]

This passage clearly implies the possibility of gradations in the I-Thou encounters. The encounter of a musical neophyte with Beethoven's Seventh Symphony, rich though it may be, is less rich than that of a trained musician. Although the musician may not consciously struggle to bring his critical knowledge to bear upon the performance (if he does, he will not encounter the music as his Thou), it is there and operating all the same. While this technical knowledge makes it harder for the musician to "let himself go" at a concert, his Thou encounters, when they occur, will be just that much richer. Only one who has actually mastered a discipline, can witness to the deeper fulfillment of subsequent Thou encounters. As Buber puts it, "It is not as though scientific and aesthetic understanding were not necessary; but they are necessary to man that he may do his work with precision and plunge it in the truth of relation, which is above the understanding and gathers it up in itself." [44]

This point too is not objectively demonstrable. Expanding on Buber's hint we may say that I-It knowledge does enrich the I-Thou encounter but there is no way of demonstrating it because one cannot demonstrate the worth of an artistic discipline to the obdurate philistine. He will not endure the dryness of the training, therefore he never reaches the point at which the deeper gratifications are to be found. Similarly, when confronted with the man of critical intelligence who holds back in face of the very possibility of fresh experience — confining himself to the domain of objective knowledge over which his control is secure — there is no way of demonstrating the meanings disclosed in the realm of Thou. "Only he reaches the meaning," Buber declares, "who stands firm, without holding back or reservation, before the whole might of reality and answers it in a living way." [45]

In speaking of "meaning" within the context of his philosophy of dialogue Buber refers to something that is at once concrete and elusive. It is elusive because, like the I-Thou relation, it cannot be defined, it can only be indicated. It is concrete because, meaning, for Buber, is a facet of specific Thou encounters. It separates music from noise, poetry from words, sculpture from shape. It is also concrete because it is immediate. The meaning conveyed by Beethoven's Seventh Symphony is musical; it cannot be expressed in words any more than the full meaning of a poem can be expressed in critical prose.[46] "That meaning is open and accessible in the actual lived concrete does not mean it is to be won and possessed through any type of analytical or synthetic investigation or through any type of reflection upon the lived concrete. Meaning is to be experienced in living action and suffering itself, in the unreduced immediacy of the moment." [47]

Conceptual language cannot capture the meanings of the I-Thou encounters in propositional form; but it can provide information which enriches them, and it is successful insofar as it succeeds in this task. The reason that critical issues in art are never conclusively resolved lies in the disparity between their language and the nature of the concrete encounters whose meaning they seek to interpret. A critic reviewing a Beethoven performance may write in objective terms about tempi and other technical matters, thereby creating the illusion of a definitive statement; but the final test is the meeting of I and Thou in the name of which music is both composed and performed, and this is never objective or definitive. So too, while every great painter uncovers an aspect of reality that would not have become visible unless his eyes had beheld it, Buber notes that, ". . . it is not something that existed in itself outside these eyes; it is a reality of relation, the product of a meeting. The painter lives in an immeasurable multiplicity and diversity of these aspects, to none of which, nor to all of them taken together, can the character of an absolute perception be ascribed. The situation is not essentially different with regard to philosophy." [48] For which reason Buber concludes that there can be no absolute knowledge which can set a single philosophy in place of the contending systems.[49]

Buber's language stands closer to the immediacies of relation than does that of most philosophers. He uses existential language to call attention to dimensions of existence that we often experience but fail to notice. His thought deepens our recollections of previous I-Thou encounters and points the way to new ones. In the end, the many insights combine into a unified perspective, so that his philosophy of dialogue itself stands before us as a Thou.

3. The Eternal Thou and the Living God

> In every sphere in its own way, through each process of becoming that is present to us we look out toward the fringe of the eternal Thou; in each we are aware of a breath from the eternal Thou; in each Thou we address the eternal Thou.[1]

We address the eternal Thou in each Thou because, through the meaning that emerges out of the I-Thou encounters of everyday life, man comes upon an overarching framework of meaning that enables him to live in the cosmos as in a home. Buber might well adapt Plato's analogy of the sun to explain the relation of the encounter with the eternal Thou to other I-Thou encounters. As the sun is at once the most visible of objects and the source of the light that enables all other objects to become visible, so God, the eternal Thou, is at once the supreme partner of the dialogue and the power underlying all other I-Thou encounters.

We recognize the eternal Thou as the ground of all I-Thou encounters because of the total framework of meaning that is manifest when we "let go" and enter into a relation. The approach to relation with the eternal Thou is given in the baffling teaching of Jesus: "Whosoever shall seek to save his life shall lose it; and whosoever shall lose his life shall preserve it" (Lk 17:33). It is the character of the seeking that makes the difference. Overanxious preoccupation with the meaning of one's own existence can only lead to the kind of intense introspection that sets one still further away from genuine relations to the world. By contrast, the man who responds without excessive self-consciousness to the beings over against him finds the meaning of his own life. "It is a finding without seeking. . . . His sense of Thou, which cannot be satiated till he finds the endless Thou, had the Thou present to it from the beginning; the presence had only to become wholly real to him in the reality of the hallowed life of the world." [2]

In an encounter with a tree we come to see it as a being existing in its own right, independent of human purposes. More than this, we come to see it as a creation of God, who creates and sustains all beings in the universe, including ourselves. The musician, in the cumulative effect of many encounters with "spiritual beings" in the third sphere of encounter, may come to an apprehension of a total perspective in which his life as a musician, and as a man, is set. "He who enters on the absolute relation [with the eternal Thou] is concerned with nothing isolated anymore, neither things nor beings, neither earth nor heaven; but everything is gathered up in the relation." [3]

Yet God is far more than the total of I-Thou encounters in the world. "Every sphere is compassed in the eternal Thou, but it is not compassed in them." [4] God is manifest to man as the supreme partner of the I-Thou encounter because, ". . . God is the Being that is directly, most nearly, and lastingly, over against us, that may properly only be addressed not expressed." [5] A great Rabbi, irked at a disciple who would not answer the question, "What do we mean when we say 'God'?" demanded a reason for his refusal. The disciple said, "Because I do not know." The master replied, "Do you think I know? But I must say it, for it is so, and therefore I must say it: He is definitely there, and except for Him nothing is definitely there—and this is He." [6]

The encounters with the eternal Thou are like all I-Thou encounters; the presence of the other is the bearer of meaning, but they yield no objective contents. Buber uses an analogy from the domain of art to explain the sense in which we may speak of one God when all we experience is a sequence of encounters. To understand a poem we must let it speak to us in its own unique terms. But when we read a series of poems by the same author, we understand more than the individual poems, we come to an understanding of the poet. "In such a way, out of the givers of the signs, the speakers of the words in lived life, out of the moment Gods there arises for us with a single identity the Lord of the voice, the One." [7]

The one God emerges from the many encounters with the eternal Thou but as Thou, not as an object. His nature cannot be fixed in propositional forms. "The religious reality of the meeting with the Meeter, who shines through all forms and is Himself formless, knows no image of Him, nothing comprehensible as object. It knows only the presence of the Present One." [8] As there can, according to Buber, be no objective criterion of knowledge that will resolve the traditional problems of judgment that engage the attention of philosophers, so there can be no objective knowledge that will resolve the ancient disputes of the theologians.

In spite of his mistrust of conceptualizing approaches to God, Buber presents his views in philosophical terms. He would not be understood when speaking directly in religious language, since our world is a secular one whose thought patterns have been shaped by the objectifying and abstracting tendencies of philosophy. Religious language is related to philosophical language as Buber's philosophy of dialogue is related to systems of philosophy which are involved in the I-It posture. Religious language seeks to remain close to the concrete immediacies of experience. "Philosophy is grounded on the presupposition that one sees the absolute in universals. In opposition to this, religion, when it has to define itself philosophically, says that it means the covenant of the absolute with the particular, with the concrete." [9]

Buber also speaks of the relation between religion and philosophy as that between a meeting with the divine and its objectification in thought.[10] It is the difference, in Pascal's classic formulation, between the God of Abraham, Isaac, and Jacob and the God of the Philosophers and scholars. Whatever Pascal may have thought on the subject, Buber is certain that the theologians belong with the philosophers and scholars, "The God of the theologians too, is a logicized God. . . . " [11] Theologians adopt the I-It posture in their effort to incorporate God into objective systems of thought. In doing so, they hope to provide religion with a continuity that will make it independent of the ephemeral character of man's encounters with the eternal Thou. They can succeed in this effort, but only at the price of imposing the limitations of human concepts upon One who is limitless.

Although he is sharply critical of theology, Buber has exerted an enormous influence upon its contemporary practitioners because he has pointed the way to a fresh approach to perennial difficulties of the theological enterprise. To appreciate this, we must briefly consider two fundamental types of theology, the confessional and the apologetic.

Confessional theology, Luther's is a notable instance,

attempts to clarify the meaning of the Faith to those who stand within the religious community. It does so in language that is reflective, but which, at the same time, tries to remain as close as possible to the concrete experiences of the faithful. In this sense, it is similar to the philosophy of dialogue. But it is far more limited, since it operates within a framework of religious dogma and does not attempt to fashion an independent philosophical approach to reality. For this reason, it rarely makes any impact outside the circle of believers.

Apologetic theologians, such as Aquinas, address the non-believers as well as the faithful. They defend the Faith against philosophical criticism in an effort to demonstrate its reasonable character. To this end, they have generally adopted the philosophical styles of their day; therefore Buber can, with some justice, accuse them of logicizing God, since Western philosophy has been dominated by objective approaches to reality. What is more, their use of these approaches has placed apologetic theologians at a severe disadvantage, which can best be appreciated by considering a specific issue such as anthropomorphism.

Philosophers persistently criticize religions that speak of a personal God for being blatantly anthropomorphic. By this the philosophers mean that talk of God as person involves the attribution of human form to that which is not human; or, in a broader sense, anthropomorphism involves the interpretation of non-human phenomena by means of categories which are only properly applied to the human sphere. Some philosophers have put it pungently by noting that if triangles could form an idea of God it would be triangular, whereas cows would envisage a bovine deity.

In accepting the objective modes of thinking employed

by their critics, apologetic theologians have faced the fearsome task of establishing the personal character of the absolute by means of categories that are incapable of doing justice to the full dimension of the personal as we encounter it in everyday existence. It is no wonder that theological arguments often involve arbitrary projections of the personal onto a cosmos that the theologians themselves have presented in impersonal terms. Philosophers often suspect that it is not reason which produces the theistic conclusions of theological arguments, but the prejudicial loyalties of the theologians to the dogmatic formulations of the religious traditions they represent.

Buber cannot be accused of employing anthropomorphic arguments in a desperate attempt to shore up religious dogma. He stands apart from apologetic theology, not only in his drive to eschew objective demonstration and confine himself to existential evocation but also in the over-all consistency of his outlook. In his approach to every facet of reality, the deepest meanings arise out of the attitude of personal engagement. The explicitly religious dimension, represented by the encounter with the eternal Thou, is organically related to the rest; it is the supreme and all-encompassing instance of meaningful relation.

Buber's specific refutation of the philosophical charge that the personal God of religion represents a form of anthropomorphism, is directed against the thought of Spinoza, which he considers the greatest anti-anthropomorphic effort undertaken by man. Spinoza attempted to purify God from the strain of being open to human address, because a God who could be spoken to was not lofty enough for him. In place of the living God of Israel he set a pantheism that identified the divine with the creative ground of the universe. "Spinoza's fundamental mistake," Buber claims, "was that he imagined the teaching of Israel to mean that God is a person; and he turned against this as a lessening of the Godhead. But the truth of the teaching lies in its insistence that God is *also* a person; and that stands over against all impersonal, unapproachable 'purity' on the part of God as a heightening of the Godhead." [12]

Spinoza regarded the universe as an infinity of divine attributes of which man apprehends two, extension and intellect, or, as Buber understands them, nature and spirit. To these, says Buber, talking for the moment in Spinoza's terms, must be added a third, and no less fundamental one — the personal.[13] This emphasis on the personal as a unique mode of being — not reducible to nature, spirit, or to any combination of the two — is a central theme of Buber's thought, and of existentialism.

Buber carries his analysis one step further. He notes that there is a point at which Spinoza's thought breaks through the sphere of discursive thinking to that of religious actuality. This is in his talk of the "intellectual love of God." To be sure, Spinoza regards this as God's love of Himself, since he identifies God with the universe. Nevertheless, notes Buber, in Spinoza's system, ". . . God — the very God among the infinity of whose attributes nature and spirit are only two — loves, and since His love becomes manifest in our love of Him the divine love must be of the same essence as human love." [14] But if this is so, then Spinoza's own talk of love between the divine and the human, regardless of the extent to which he endeavors to qualify it as purely "intellectual," witnesses to the directness of personal encounter between man and God. "For when man learns to love God," says Buber, "he senses an actuality which rises above the idea. Even if he makes the philosopher's great effort to sustain the object of his love as an object of his philosophical thought, the love itself bears witness to the existence of the Beloved." [15]

Buber insists that the encounter with God is real and not illusory because to encounter the eternal Thou, ". . . the world of sense does not need to be laid aside as though it were illusory. There is no illusory world, there is only the world — which appears to us as twofold in accordance with our twofold attitude." [16] Because God is only encountered in the I-Thou attitude, we cannot know Him as "He-is-in-Himself." We may speak of Him as person, though only symbolically, because again and again, in the transitory encounters, He stands over against us as person. "It is indeed legitimate to speak of the person of God within the religious relation and its language; but in doing so we are making no statement about the absolute which reduces it to the personal." [17]

Symbols are necessary because all communication depends upon the conventional representations of experience they achieve. But Buber warns us that symbols of the divine tend to be used in a literal and objective way, so that finally, they cease to point to the God of encounter. "Symbols of God come into being . . . they are set before the community of believers in plastic or theological forms. . . . Yet they always quickly desire to be more than they are, more than signs and pointers toward Him. It finally happens ever again that they swell themselves up and obstruct the way to Him, and he removes Himself from them." [18] By speaking of the "eternal Thou," a symbol that, as set in the context of his philosophy of dialogue, expresses the transitory character of man's relation to God, Buber hopes to avoid that pitfall and remain true to the reality of encounter.

His attempt to remain close to the immediacies of encounter while speaking in philosophical terms leads Buber to employ paradoxes. As he uses them, they involve the simultaneous affirmation of two propositions which, from the standpoint of detached rationality, are regarded as being incompatible with each other. But reality does not confront man in propositional form. "It is only when reality is turned into logic and A and non-A dare no longer dwell together, that we get determinism and indeterminism, a doctrine of predestination and a doctrine of freedom, each excluding the other. According to the logical conception of truth only one of two contraries can be true, but in the reality of life as one lives it they are inseparable." [19]

Once again, Buber's thought reveals an over-all consistency that makes it a potent force for the understanding of religion. He does not use *ad hoc* procedures, in this case the category of paradox, in an attempt to substantiate religious dogmas. The paradox of freedom and determinism stands at the heart of every I-Thou encounter. The Thou cannot be found by seeking, yet it cannot be found without it. From a propositional standpoint, a contradiction is involved, but in the immediacy of the encounter itself, man knows that ". . . the relation means being chosen and choosing, suffering and action in one . . ." [20] The paradoxes of transcendence-immanence, grace-freedom, and the others which characterize the religions, are only special cases. "The religious communication of a content of being takes place in paradox. It is not demonstrable assertion . . . but a pointing toward the hidden realm of existence of the hearing man himself and that which is to be experienced there and there alone."[21]

It is the reality of his own experience and not the demands of religious dogma that leads Buber to assert the paradoxes of religion. In using them he has been influenced by the teachings of the Jewish tradition, but not in a sterile and rigid way. "Even when the individual calls an absolute criterion handed down by religious tradition his own, it must be reforged in the fire of the truth of his personal essential relation to the absolute if it is to win true validity."[22]

He has been influenced by the paradoxical utterances of the great religious figures of Judaism, such as the Rabbi who sang, "My God, where can I find you, but where can I not find you?"[23] He has been influenced by the Jews of Eastern Europe who addressed God with the awful name *Ribbono Shel Olam*, Lord of the World, and with the name *Gottenyu*, which literally means "Our God," and is formed, after the fashion of Yiddish (that blend of Hebrew, of medieval German, and of the language of any locality in which Jews find themselves) by the combination of the German word for God with the Hebrew suffix meaning "our." Only one who has heard it uttered by Jewish lips in the joys and agonies of day-to-day living can appreciate the tenderness that transformed the suffix "*nyu*" into an affectionate diminutive, and the name *Gottenyu* into a term of familiar intimacy. It is the experiences involved in the use of these two names of God rather than any form of Jewish dogmatics that enable Buber to exclaim: "Of course God is the 'wholly Other'; but He is also the wholly Same, the wholly Present. Of course He is the *Mysterium Tremendum* that appears and overthrows; but He is also the mystery of the self-evident, nearer to me than my *I*."[24]

Buber, as we have seen, says that we cannot know "God-in-Himself." We can only know Him as a person, because that is the way He encounters us in relation. Yet the attempt to communicate religious reality in the language of philosophy raises a further problem. Persons as we know them are limited whereas God, as we encounter Him, is without limit. This leads Buber to talk of the "absolute Person" we call God. "Can this," he says, "be taken to mean that God 'is' a personality? The absolute character of His personality, that paradox of paradoxes, prohibits any such statement. It only means that God loves as a personality and that He wishes to be loved like a personality." [25]

Some theologians who are impressed with the power of Buber's evocation of God as person have misused his thought by suggesting that the encounter with the eternal Thou is a special intuition of mysteries. Buber, however, regards the encounter with God as one that takes place in, and illumines, life in its everyday aspects. Indeed, his views on the eternal Thou are expressed in the context of an explicit rejection of that most exotic form of intuition — mysticism — and this by one who claims to have known the raptures of its rare moments of exaltation. By the time he wrote *I and Thou*, Buber had come to regard the central reality of the ordinary hour in which a streak of sun shines on a maple twig and provides a glimpse of the eternal Thou, as a deeper encounter with being than that of all the complicated enigmas of the mystical approach in which the self and the absolute are merged.[26]

He was disillusioned with mysticism because the unity of absorption in which the self and the absolute are one is inevitably succeeded by the duality of self and world. Furthermore, the unity experienced in mystical ecstasy can by its very nature have no bearing on earthly cares, because the world itself has no part in the unity experienced — the mystics shed worldly concerns in their efforts to achieve it. "If that abundantly rich heavenly moment has nothing to do with my poor earthly moment — what has it then to do with me, who have still to live, in all seriousness still to live, on earth? Thus are the masters to be understood who have renounced the raptures of ecstatic 'union.' "[27] In our day, the foremost among these masters is Buber himself.

Some admirers of Buber's thought are happy to talk about the eternal Thou but are loath to speak of God. The former, is a term that is somewhat fashionable as intellectual currency, whereas, "God" is associated with religion "and all that." Nothing could be further from Buber's intention than the use of the philosophy of dialogue as a form of *avant-garde* intellectuality. Buber uses the term "eternal Thou" in order to emphasize the non-objective character of the divine-human encounter and to stress its continuity with the encounters of everyday life. In using it, he hopes to overcome the inhibitions induced in his readers by the prejudices of contemporary culture, so that they will "let go" and enter into relation with the God whom they meet on the fringe of all the I-Thou encounters they experience. But he has no intention of substituting the term "eternal Thou" for the word "God." When a philosopher rebuked him for using the word "God," on the grounds that it had been so much abused through the centuries that it was almost blasphemous to use it, Buber passionately replied:

> Yes, it is the most heavy-laden of all human words. None has become so soiled, so mutilated. Just for this reason I may not abandon it. Generations of men have laid the burden of their anxious lives upon this word and weighed it to the ground; it

> lies in the dust and bears their whole burden. The races of man with their religious factions have torn the word to pieces; they have killed for it and died for it, and it bears their finger-marks and their blood. Where might I find a word like it to describe the highest! If I took the purest, most sparkling concept from the inner treasure-chamber of the philosophers, I could only capture thereby an unbinding product of thought. I could not capture the presence of Him whom the generations of men have honored and degraded with their awesome living and dying.

This note of affirming men, all men, in their search for God in opposition to the philosopher's quest for conceptual purity with regard to the divine, then reaches a crescendo.

> I do indeed mean Him whom the hell-tormented and heaven-storming generations of men mean. Certainly, they draw caricatures and write "God" underneath; they murder one another and say "in God's name." But when all madness and delusion fall to dust, when they stand over against Him in the loneliest darkness and no longer say "He, He" but rather sigh "Thou," shout "Thou," all of them the one word, and when they then add "God," is it not the real God whom they all implore, the One living God, the God of the children of man? Is it not He who *hears* them? And just for this reason is not the word "God," the word of appeal, the word which has become a *name*, consecrated in all human tongues for all times? [28]

Buber esteems those who would refrain from using the word "God" because it has been so fearfully exploited, but he feels that they are misguided. All the reticence induced by their concern for purity will not restore the absolute to its proper role in human affairs. To accomplish this purpose, we must plunge fully into the responsibilities of each hour, using the name of God, but fighting against its exploitation by ourselves and others. "We cannot cleanse the word 'God' and we cannot make it whole; but, defiled and mutilated as it is, we can raise it from the ground and set it over an hour of great care." [29]

A critic has complained that this sort of talk leaves the matter where it previously stood, for the powerful rhetoric of the philosophy of dialogue uses language so close to the immediacy of encounter that Buber can only address those who have already achieved the awareness he wishes to elicit.[30] There is a measure of truth in this. Those who have an explicitly religious outlook on life respond most readily to the language of *I and Thou.* But the critic's suggestion that Buber might do better to abandon the evocative language of his dialogic approach and adopt a sober form of expression that would address those who are recalcitrant toward religion is, in effect, a demand that he abandon the truth as he sees it.

Buber's thought has no objective content. He does not think it possible for man to achieve knowledge that would conclusively resolve the most significant questions of existence. The content of his thought is conveyed in immediate language which points to the meanings disclosed to man in the posture of engagement. Answers are given, but not in objective terms: "I myself," he writes, "have no 'doctrine.' My function is to point out realities of this order. He who expects of me a teaching other than a pointing out of this character, will always be disillusioned." [31]

Dialogic thinking may confirm the explicitly religious

person in his faith. It may evoke an explicit recognition of faith in one who had experienced, but not acknowledged, the encounter with the eternal Thou. Finally, it may shake the complacency of a life lived in the fixed and secure paths of objective knowledge and confront it with "the venture of the infinite." [32] But it cannot coerce anyone into adopting its perspectives. The demand that Buber achieve a mode of address that will enable him to open hearts that are closed to the living God is another form of the demand that he produce the magic talisman of the objective criterion of knowledge.

Buber has an answer to modern thinkers who deny the reality of the divine-human encounter. It is, however, not an objective refutation; it is a penetrating suggestion arising out of his analysis of contemporary culture. He regards solipsism as the greatest enemy of the spirit. As he uses this conception, it means swallowing reality — which is only to be met in contact with other beings — into the inner recesses of the self. In the first sphere of encounter, our life with nature, it is only the psychotic who seriously attempts to live this doctrine by behaving in a way that denies the reality of tangible bodies. In the second sphere, life between man and man, it is the extreme neurotic who lives solipsistically by acting as if love were no more than a function of his ego. Psychotherapy tries to heal the wounds he has suffered so that he can "let go" and enter into the life of love, which of course, involves the risk that he may again be hurt. Here Buber is in accord with the therapists; he who avoids this risk is less than a man.

In the third sphere, the sphere of the spirit — where men are confronted with the unconditional demand of morality, with the values embodied in art, and with our ideals — it is our age itself that is sick. Under the influence of thinkers who invoke the prestige of science in support of questionable philosophical judgments, we relegate values to the level of subjective feelings. Furthermore, many people who encounter the reality of God in their lives are inhibited from affirming Him by some of the most fashionable teachings of our era. Freud's notion of "wish-fulfillment" and Jung's view of the "archetypes" reduce the reality of the eternal Thou standing over against the self into "human, all too human" functions of the psyche.

Against these views Buber argues that, "Not only statements about God, but all statements in general are 'human.' Yet is anything positive or negative thereby ascertained about their truth? The distinction which is here in question is thus not that between psychic and non-psychic statements, but that between psychic statements to which a superpsychic reality corresponds and psychic statements to which none corresponds." [33]

That Buber regards God as a superpsychic reality is obvious from the "God-intoxicated" character of everything he writes. He has directed a singularly pungent retort to Max Stirner (1806–1856), another of the modern exponents of the view that God is an illusion that man projects onto reality: "Ignorant of the reality whose appearance is the appearance, he proves its nature to be appearance." [34]

The malady of our age is intensified because the success of science has led men to apply the technique of experimentation to all human problems. But the deepest levels of meaning can only be encountered in the I-Thou relation which involves an element of spontaneity that is precluded by experimentation.

> In our age the I-It relation, gigantically swollen, has usurped, practically uncontested, the mastery and the rule. The I of this relation, an I that possesses all, makes all, succeeds with all, this I that is unable to say Thou, unable to meet a being essentially, is the lord of the hour. This selfhood that has become omnipotent, with all the It around it, can naturally acknowledge neither God nor any genuine absolute which manifests itself to men as of non-human origin. It steps between and shuts off from us the light of heaven.[35]

The prescription that accompanies this diagnosis shows Buber to be one of the wise men of our age. Religious thinkers have become very much aware of the fact that all men, believers or not, have an ultimate value, an absolute, in the name of which they live. Nation, party, power, knowledge, money — all are capable of being made into an idol. It is, therefore, a great temptation for them to suppose that if they show a man the conditioned nature of his false absolute, that is, if they shatter his idol, he will then turn to the true absolute, to God. But they fail to see that idolatry is as much a matter of attitude as it is of object. Before making a judgment as to the authenticity with which a man held any world-view whatever, Buber would ask the following questions: "Does a world-view dwell in the head or in the whole man? Does it live only in the hours of proclamation or also in the silent private periods of his life? Does he use it or does he give himself to it?" [36]

Buber's prescription involves a change in the character as well as in the object of worship. The man who has used a cause or a value as a means of inflating his ego or of attaining his own security will not alter this pattern merely by shifting his devotion to the living God. In fact, too many adherents of religion employ their belief in God as a means of assuring themselves a secure berth in heaven rather than as a challenge to work here and now for the realization of His kingdom. To enter into authentic relation with God, the idolator must do more than alter his attitude toward God, he must change his mode of relating himself to each and every being that confronts him. He must affirm other beings as existing in their own right and must not suppress the element of spontaneity that is possible in his relations with them. If he fails to do this, regardless of the religious position he espouses, he will remain immersed in the world of It, calculating the utility of other beings, and of God as well.[37]

Buber presented this analysis long before the manifestation of that familiar pattern of our times, conversions from the absolute of the Communist Party to the absolute of religious faith. In all too many cases, the converts exhibit the very characteristic Buber derided, the substitution of the object without the change in attitude. Many observers of this phenomenon have advanced the glib explanation that converts from Communism to religion are "types" who need one absolute or another. The comments have been particularly caustic when the converts have espoused Roman Catholicism. But what the critics forget is that all men, including these critics themselves, are "types" who need an ultimate value for their lives.

Buber's crucial point must again be emphasized: "Certainly what one believes is important, but still more important is how one believes it."[38] A man may leave the Communist Party and be converted to Roman Catholicism, or he may be converted to a form of liberal religion which bitterly opposes Catholicism, he may even espouse a philosophical position which denies the possibility of there being an absolute; and, in defending any of these new positions, he may still conduct himself in the way that characterized his operations within the Party. On the other hand, he may leave the Party and change his posture toward the world along with his ideology. Should he fail to effect a change in posture, far from acquiring the humility that characterizes the authentic man of faith, the philosopher, or the scientist, he will continue to regard any position he happens to hold as the last word. "In a genuine dialogue," says Buber, "each of the partners, even when he stands in opposition to the other, heeds, affirms, and confirms his opponent as an existing other." [39] But the man who is converted from the Party to religion without changing his way of relating himself to the absolute will be incapable of genuine dialogue. He will persist in the patterns of ideological warfare and regard all opponents as dangerous enemies of truth to be annhilated in argument and eleminated from social influence.

> He who has been converted by this substitution of objects now "holds" a phantom that he calls God. But God, the eternal Presence, does not permit Himself to be held. Woe to the man so possessed that he thinks he possesses God! [40]

God cannot be possessed; He can only be encountered. The encounters with the eternal Thou constitute the root experiences of the phenomenon theologians call "revelation." The term is intended to suggest the divine initiative. Revelation does not involve the cultivation of a capacity which is latent in man, but God's self-disclosure in the midst of personal relation with men. This sense of "an initiative not our own" corresponds to other aspects of experience. "One can believe in and accept a meaning or value, one can set it as a guiding light over one's life if one has discovered it, not if one has invented it. It can be for me an illuminating meaning, a direction-giving value only if it has been revealed to me in my meeting with Being. . . ." [41]

As the encounters with the eternal Thou are but special cases of the I-Thou encounters of everyday life, similarly, "The mighty revelations to which the religions appeal are like in being with the quiet revelations that are to be found everywhere and at all times." [42] They yield the same overwhelming sense of meaningful presence; they provide a vision of the world as it ought to be; and a powerful impetus to action which will bring the world we live in into conformity with that vision.[43] "Every religious utterance is a vain attempt to do justice to the meaning which has been attained. . . . The meaning is found through the engagement of one's own person; it only reveals itself as one takes part in its revelation." [44]

The difference between the mighty revelations that give birth to new religions and the everyday encounters with the eternal Thou is an important one, but it is one of degree. Paul Tillich, the contemporary Protestant theologian, expresses it clearly in his distinction between original and dependent revelation. Original revelation represents a fundamentally new approach to reality which creates a new context of meaning. Dependent revelation involves the renewal of the original experience on the part of followers who elaborate the meanings disclosed to the founders of the faith. "While Peter encountered the man Jesus whom he called the Christ in an original revelatory ecstasy, following generations," says Tillich, "met the Jesus who had been received as the Christ by Peter and the other apostles." [45]

Revelation is not a form of knowledge which explains the

inner workings of a hitherto baffling phenomenon as when scientists discover the reasons for the terrifying phenomenon of volcanic eruption; revelation is like a glimpse into the character of someone we love — the illumination is intense, but the mystery of otherness persists.

> All religious reality begins with what biblical religion calls the "fear of God." It comes when our existence between birth and death becomes incomprehensible and uncanny, when all security is shattered through the mystery. This is not the relative mystery of that which is inaccessible only to the present state of human knowledge and is hence in principle discoverable. It is the essential mystery, the inscrutableness of which belongs to its very nature; it is the unknowable.[46]

Integral to Buber's understanding of the relation between God and man is the conviction — which follows on the inscrutable character of the mystery — that, ". . . the living God is not only a self-revealing but also a self-concealing God."[47] This serves as a protest against any religion or theology that exhausts the mystery in dogmatic or systematic formulations. And Buber expresses this protest by means of a verse which — since he returns to it again and again — he undoubtedly regards as a key to the Bible: "Verily Thou art a God that hidest thyself, O God of Israel, the Saviour" (Is 45:15).

Speaking of a hiding as well as a revealing God is a way of pointing to the mystery of dialogue itself — to the alternation between the sense of God's nearness and of His remoteness. For years Buber has groped for images which would enable him to express this mystery. The images he has actually used have not been consistent. A number of them focus the responsibility for the disruption of the dialogue on man alone. "The waves of the aether roar on always, but for most of the time we have turned off our receivers." [48] Again he says, "Often enough we think there is nothing to hear, but long before we have ourselves put wax in our ears." [49] In another context we find him using an image which does not unequivocally focus the blame for the disruption on the human will, but which suggests that it is human willing which must see to it that communication between God and man is resumed. "Its light seems darkened only because the eye suffers from a cataract. . . ." [50]

The underlying conviction expressed by these images is the unswerving faithfulness of God. This conviction is also the basis of Buber's assertion that, "The eternal Thou can by its nature not become an It. . . ."; that God is always ready to address man as a Thou.[51] This is not an exception to his prohibition against fixing God in conceptual terms, but is an existential affirmation grounded in the immediacy of encounter — and there alone. But man, he continues, cannot bear the insecurity of the life-rhythm of relation: he tries to fix the divine in unchanging images. "And yet in accordance with our nature we are continually making the eternal Thou into It, into some thing — making God into a thing." [52]

But the indictment of man expressed in these images is too facile a way of dealing with this mystery, and in other contexts Buber — at least implicitly — acknowledges this. The suggestion that we need only "remove the wax from our ears" in order to hear the voice of God must be contrasted with his image of the "eclipse of God," which suggests something that has taken place between God and man, rather than in man alone. "Eclipse of the light of heaven, eclipse of God —

such indeed is the character of the historic hour through which the world is passing. But it is not a process which can be adequately accounted for by instancing the changes that have taken place in man's spirit."[53] The image of the "eclipse" is more satisfactory than the others because it does justice to the paradoxical character of encounter, the ". . . being chosen and choosing, suffering and action in one. . . ."[54] It takes account of the appalling misery of those who seek God and do not find Him.

Buber cannot, nor does he attempt to, offer a panacea for dispelling the darkness. He exhorts men to awareness of their absorption in the clichés of the hour which shut off the possibility of their being open to fresh experience. After achieving this awareness they may be empowered to break through to relation with the eternal Thou. But there is no guarantee — there is only the hope.

> God can never become an object for me; I can attain no other relation to Him than that of the I to its eternal Thou, that of the Thou to its eternal I. But if man is no longer able to attain this relation, if God is silent toward him and he toward God, then something has taken place, not in human subjectivity but in Being itself. It would be worthier not to explain it to oneself in sensational and incompetent sayings, such as that of the "death" of God, but to endure it as it is and at the same time to move existentially toward a new happening, toward that event in which the word between heaven and earth will again be heard.[55]

At this point, even the most sympathetic reader might be oppressed by a feeling that Buber's thinking degenerates into obscurantism. After all, this mystery of the hiding God seems to envelop in darkness that which the mystery of the revealing

God disclosed, or as Buber has put it, "His revelation is nothing but a different form of hiding His face." [56] In a recent collection of essays relating contemporary philosophical trends to theology, Basil Mitchell uses a parable which sheds some light on this issue.

In an occupied country a partisan is confronted by a stranger who claims to be the head of the resistance movement to which the partisan belongs. In a night of intense conversation he gains the faith of the partisan who undertakes to trust him no matter what happens. This faith is put to the test when the stranger reappears as head of the police forces of the occupying power. The faithful one assures his comrades that the stranger is really "one of us" — that he is using his position in the police to confound the enemy. When the stranger intervenes in mysterious ways to save the lives of some of the partisans, the interpretation of the faithful one is supported. On other occasions, when the stranger is instrumental in the capture of some of the partisans, the faithful one — who no longer has direct access to the stranger — persists in his trust and assures his furious comrades that the stranger must behave in this way or his role as leader of the underground will be discovered by the enemy.[57]

The parable enables us to understand the considerations which lead Buber to talk of the revealing and hiding God. There are relations which are so subtle that they resist all attempts to define them by means of propositions that can be verified by experimental tests. One of these is the kind of trust the partisan reposes in the mysterious stranger. It stands at the heart of both love and faith. Yet neither love nor faith need be blind; both may judge actions — of the beloved or of the one in whom faith is reposed — as counting for or against trustworthiness. However, to devise a conclusive test of either love or faith — for example, if God does not answer this prayer then I can no longer believe in Him — is to show that the trust that is a necessary condition of these relations has already been destroyed. Buber's talk of God as "self-revealing and also self-concealing" is an attempt to convey the external counterpart of this inner dimension of trust. But, of course, he cannot prove the existence of the external counterpart — it is only manifest as the Presence which stands over against the self in the immediacy of encounter.

As Buber's thought matured in the direction of the philosophy expressed in *I and Thou,* it increasingly interacted with the Old Testament. There he found the consummate record of "The dialogue between heaven and earth." [58] In it the alternation between the revealing and hiding God, between encounter and its disruption, finds its clearest expression. The dialogue between God and Israel is not to be understood as a dramatic façade which lends color to the enduring cultural values — monotheism, the demand for social justice, the sabbath, and the rest — contributed to mankind by this people; it is itself the substance of the religious reality which enkindled its life.

> The great achievement of Israel is not so much that it has told mankind of the one, real God, the origin and goal of all that exists, but rather that it has taught men that they can address this God in very reality, that men can say Thou to Him, that we human beings can stand face to face with Him, that there is communion between God and man.[59]

4. The Man of Today and the Jewish Bible

IN our day, the dissolution of cherished assumptions and traditional values has resulted in a painful groping for faith. Many voices call for a return to the bulwarks of times gone by, and no bulwark has been more imposing than the Bible. But an approach to the Bible based on this sort of thinking can only result in reactionary attempts to impose the outmoded dogmas of former eras on the ever-expanding vitalities of contemporary life.

Martin Buber makes no appeal for a "return" to the Bible. He never returned to it himself — in the sense of a "return" based upon a sense of guilt at having deserted the faith of the fathers, or motivation of a similar character.[1] As his thought developed he found in the Jewish Bible the most meaningful record of man's response to the full dimension of life and history. He calls it, interchangeably, the "Jewish" or "Hebrew" Bible — rejecting the common designation, the Old Testament, as a complete misnomer, since it is neither "old" in the sense of being superseded, nor a testament.

Buber's approach is avowedly interpretative and selective: ". . . I never said I accepted the Hebrew Bible as a whole — far from it. In my choice I am led by what I can, concentrating my whole being on it, believe as willed by God for me, for us, for man. I never pretended to have another criterion and I do not think there is another. I invite my readers to act accordingly."[2]

This certainly does not set Buber apart from the main stream of the Western religious tradition. From the time the worshippers of the living God of Israel first encountered the critical mentality of the Greek philosophers, religious thinkers have had to maintain the validity of biblical revelation without being able to recapture the naïveté of the biblical accounts in which the voice of the Lord thunders from the clouds. Furthermore, each generation has found it necessary to select from and interpret the texts in order to relate the Scriptures to the concrete situations in which the faithful have found themselves. But in his efforts to engage in this venerable enterprise of selection and interpretation Buber has the advantage of approaching the Bible with a philosophy that is itself intimately related to it.

While Buber has undoubtedly interpreted the Bible in terms of his philosophy of dialogue, the Jewish Bible was itself a crucial influence upon the development of that philosophy.[3] For example, he found his dialogical approach to knowledge woven into the very structure of biblical Hebrew. The statement, "Now Adam knew Eve his wife and she conceived and bore Cain . . ." (Gen 4:1), is not a euphemism that the translators concocted in order to avoid using a verb for sexual intercourse, it is a literal translation, (and no reader of the Bible could imagine that the authors of the Hebrew original were prudish). Buber finds an important principle involved in this use of the verb "to know." He notes that ". . . the original meaning of the Hebrew verb 'to recognise, to know,' in distinction from Western languages, belongs not to the sphere of reflection but to that of contact. The decisive event for 'knowing' in biblical Hebrew is not that one looks at an object, but that one comes into touch with it. This basic difference is developed in the realm of the relation of the soul to other beings, where the fact of mutuality changes everything." [4]

While his dialogical philosophy provides the interpretive framework of Buber's biblical studies, the discipline of the higher criticism of the Old Testament, whose intricacies he thoroughly mastered, provides the critical and technical milieu to which these studies are addressed. The term "higher," as distinguished from "textual," criticism is designed to reflect the daring departure of the former type in treating the Bible as a body of literature, to be examined according to the best canons of literary criticism available. Previously the Bible had been venerated as a depository of religious truth and insulated from secular study.

As practiced by its most influential exponent, Julius Wellhausen (1844–1918) and those who followed him, higher criticism was unquestionably a liberating influence. The scholars who practiced it focused on the human elements in the biblical accounts — on the factors that revealed the various books to be products of their time, and on the elements within the community of Israel that had played a role in their composition. They discarded dogmatic assumptions that had, through the centuries, confined biblical studies within rigid limits.

One of the higher critics' most far-reaching determinations was their insistence that Moses was not the author of the Pentateuch — the five books called by his name. Using all sorts of evidence — external and internal — they concluded that the Pentateuch as we have it was the product of the editorial compilations of a number of documents reflecting a variety of perspectives on the origins, history, and laws of Israel. These vary in age from a period somewhat prior to 1,000 B.C. to about 400 B.C., the probable date (according to the majority of these critics) of their final compilation. Many higher critics thought they could identify these various literary strands, even to the point of dividing individual biblical verses into fragments of different origins.

The higher critics found external evidence of the human origins of the books of Moses in the initial findings of archaeologists and of philologists devoted to deciphering the scripts and languages of the ancient Near East. In some of the materials taken from Mesopotamian civilizations, which were much older than that of Israel, they uncovered myths that seemed to be the basis for the first creation story, the story of the flood, and still others.

In addition, the higher critics found internal evidence in many parts of the biblical accounts that made it highly improbable that Moses could have been the author of the Pentateuch. For one thing, it would make the account of his death in the thirty-fourth chapter of the book of Deuteronomy ludicrous since the account ends with the statement: ". . . but no man knows the place of his burial to this day." Then there is the reference to "Dan," a locale which was not known by that name until long after the time of Moses, and a reference to an incident in Mosaic times as occurring "before Israel had a king." There are a number of other anachronisms which adherents of the traditional theory of Mosaic authorship are obliged to explain away.

Aside from anachronisms, the higher critics found a great deal of evidence for challenging the notion that the five books were the product of any *one* hand, Moses' or another's. There are stylistic differences — the sonorous sententiousness of Deuteronomy differs markedly from the other books; different accounts of the same event — the two accounts of creation with which the Bible begins; different accounts making the same point — Jacob is twice given the name Israel, at Peniel and at Bethel; and glaring inconsistencies — God tells Moses that he was not known to the Patriarchs by the name YHVH,* whereas we find that in the book of Genesis the Patriarchs did know Him by that name.

The higher critics were not the first to discover these problems. The inconsistencies that are to be found in the biblical accounts had been observed by scholars through the centuries, and, in a systematic way, by the biblical commentators of medieval Judaism. But scholars who had a supernatural world-view could dispense with these inconsistencies by giving explanations that modern man cannot use or accept. For example, scholars holding a supernatural world-view might maintain that Moses, who received so many extraordinary evidences of God's favor, could easily have foreseen the changes in various geographical designations within the land of Palestine as well as the rise of the monarchy in Israel. Therefore, it was not their discovery of the inconsistency of the biblical accounts that led Wellhausen and other higher critics to draw radical conclusions from their biblical studies; it was the development of liberal theology in Protestant, and later in Jewish, circles that produced this result.

Liberal theologians accepted the challenging implications of modern science, and especially of Newtonian physics, as these were mediated to them by the philosophical systems of Immanuel Kant and the other great thinkers who grappled

* YHVH, that most sacred name of God that is so frequently found in the Jewish Bible, is generally mispronounced Jehovah and mistranslated as "the Lord." The Jews were forbidden to speak this name, and so they substituted the word *Adonai*, meaning "my Lord," when reading the Bible aloud. Since the original Hebrew texts lacked vowels, medieval Christian Scholars were misled by this substitution into deriving the pronunciation Jehovah from the Hebrew vowels of the word Adonai.

with this development in philosophical terms. In attempting to bring their religious traditions into consonance with these developments, liberal theologians accepted the scientific assumption that the universe acted at all times according to regular, observable, and predictable patterns. These theologians rejected the view of revelation as divine self-disclosure by means of supernatural phenomena. Liberal theologians tended to focus their attention on the human side of the divine-human encounter, and in doing so, they sought the formative impulse of the biblical record in the religious consciousness of man rather than in the divine suspension of the "laws of nature." According to the liberal view, an incident such as the encounter between God and Moses at the Burning Bush could be understood as Moses' awareness of the compelling power of a will not his own, of a divine power directing him to try to liberate his fellow Hebrews from slavery. Liberal theologians regarded the details of the event, the Burning Bush, the magical staff, and the rest, as the products of the mentality of ancient man who was inclined to represent spiritual events in dramatic form. This approach enabled Christians and Jews to preserve their religious allegiance without espousing a supernatural understanding of man and the universe.

Wellhausen and his followers certainly were liberals theologically. However, at this point we should note that they did not constitute a formal school, and that the work of many higher critics, even of those who were influenced by Wellhausen, may be cited as exceptions to one or another of the points we shall direct against Wellhausen himself. Nevertheless, Wellhausen's influence has been pervasive and has led to a critical style and outlook which persist, to a degree, even today. One aspect of his outlook stood in glaring contradiction to its generally liberal tendencies. He presented the Old Testament in terms of a neat antithesis between the prophets, the spirit, and moral principles on the one hand, and the priests, "the letter of the law," and religious ritual on the other. He saw the praiseworthy prophetic tradition fulfilled in Christianity, and the sterile priestly tradition in Judaism —which he regarded as the quintessence of ritualistic religion.

This was a modern version of the traditional Christian approach to the Old Testament; Christians had always regarded it as a meritorious, indeed as a revelatory precursor of the New Testament, but only as a precursor. In the New Testament, according to the Christian view, the highest moments of the "Old" were both fulfilled and surpassed. But in the mind of Jewish scholars, the higher critics were far more galling than their predecessors in the field of Christian scholarship. Jewish scholars, who were themselves so recently freed from the ghetto and were zestfully participating in liberal European culture, could dismiss the older versions of the Christian view as part of the dogmatics of the "dark ages," but they found the higher critics extremely aggravating because the higher critics drew their invidious comparisons between the two Testaments in the name of theological liberalism, and in the name of the most advanced tendencies of "scientific" literary criticism.

A leading Jewish scholar, Solomon Schechter (1850–1915), spoke of the higher criticism of Wellhausen and his followers as a "higher anti-Semitism," that is, as a form of anti-Semitism that was culturally respectable.[5] Some higher critics may have been anti-Semitic, but Schechter's judgment of the Wellhausen theory as such was too harsh. It ignored the fact that this outlok on the Hebrew Bible and on Jewish religious history was shared, in large measure, by many Jewish intellectual leaders of the nineteenth and of the early twentieth century. It was even shared by Buber himself in the first decade of this century, although, as we shall see, he later rejected it. Schechter's judgment also ignored the fact that Christian scholars were applying the techniques of higher criticism to the New Testament with results that were devastating to many of the traditional assumptions of Christianity.

It was not anti-Semitism, but the facile liberalism of so much late ninteenth and early twentieth century thinking that blinded these scholars, Jewish and Christian alike, to the creative elements of post-biblical Judaism. They clung to the caricature of Judaism as a ceremonial and religiously sterile cult at a time when the fallacy of this caricature was being demonstrated by such Christian scholars as George F. Moore (1851–1931) and R. Travers Herford (1860–1950) and by such modern Jewish scholars as Louis Ginsberg (1873–1953), Leo Baeck (1873–1956), and Louis Finkelstein (1895–).

Buber is, as we shall have more than one occasion to note, a far from passive proponent of the Jewish cause. A large part of the critical side of his biblical studies has been directed against the distortions, oversimplifications, and misunderstandings introduced into higher criticism by the Wellhausen picture of the Jewish religion and its development. Buber's study of *Moses* restores the luster — much tarnished by the "debunking" tendencies of the critics — to this founder of the faith of Israel. He also corrects their effort to isolate the prophets from Israelite religion by setting them in an individualistic and entirely critical relation to the community. Buber's most extensive study of the Jewish Bible, *The Pro-*

phetic Faith, traces the relation of that faith to every stratum of the biblical literature from the Patriarchal narratives on through the book of Job. The prophets were unquestionably universalists whose message has carried far beyond the ears of the Hebrew people; but they were, he insists, *national* universalists who never doubted the special character of the relation between God and Israel.[6]

Buber's criticisms of the Wellhausen approach to the Jewish Bible go beyond the correction of distortions introduced by its attitude toward Judaism; he issues a more fundamental challenge to its method.

The thrill of breaking new ground generally elicits impetuous judgments from those who first establish a discipline and the higher critics were no exception. They readily challenged the traditionally accepted views of the dates and authors of the biblical books, and they were equally ready to challenge the reliability of the Hebrew texts themselves. The enterprise of emending these texts is called "textual" or "lower" criticism.

Until the discovery of the Dead Sea Scrolls,* the earliest Hebrew manuscripts of the Old Testament dated from the ninth and tenth centuries of the Christian era. But there are manuscripts of translations, for example, the Greek translation known as the Septuagint, which are dated as early as the third century of this era. Since the manuscripts of the translations were centuries older than our oldest Hebrew manuscripts, it was obvious that the Hebrew manuscripts upon which the translations were based were also several centuries older than the ninth century Hebrew manuscripts. Since

* The discovery of the Dead Sea Scrolls has yielded Hebrew biblical manuscripts centuries older than any previously known, but their discovery, after World War II, is too recent to affect our discussion of a much earlier period of higher criticism.

earlier manuscripts stand closer to the original texts and have been copied fewer times, they are presumably more reliable than recent ones. The fact that at points, especially where they are garbled, the oldest Hebrew manuscripts disagree with the early manuscripts of translations, led the higher critics to assume that the Hebrew texts available to us were not altogether reliable.

There can be no denying, on critical grounds, the conclusion that the Hebrew texts are not infallible. The difficulties connected with them had been discussed for centuries. But the "higher" critics used this result of "textual" or "lower" criticism in unrestrained fashion. Whenever they found difficulties in the Hebrew — whether of grammar, sequence, or clarity — they were ready and even eager to suggest textual alterations. In the end, the fact that a passage in the Bible conflicted with their own theories was enough to elicit conjectural emendations to the Hebrew texts on the part of many higher critics.

Before turning to the basic criticisms which Buber directs against Wellhausen and his followers, we must re-emphasize the fact that Buber is himself a higher critic. He recognizes the liberating influence of higher criticism in approaching the Jewish Bible in a spirit that is free of the trammels of centuries of dogmatic formulations. He can no more believe that Moses was the author of the books attributed to him than Wellhausen could. He does not reject, out of hand, any of the techniques employed by the critics and is especially grateful for their contributions in such areas as Hebrew grammar and biblical archaeology.

Yet Buber, while unquestionably a higher critic, is a decidedly conservative one. The reverence for the texts imparted to him by the Jewish tradition and his familiarity with the meticulous supervision that was involved in preserving and copying them made him chary of suggesting emendations. Furthermore, his respect for the concrete reality of the text itself as over against the vagueness of all critical conjectures about it reinforces this conservative tendency. While recognizing the problems a given text may present, he assumes that the men who recorded it understood what they were doing, and that we, the readers and critics, must endeavor to understand it too. We may finally be forced to alter the text, but we may not do so until we have exhausted every possibility of understanding the given form.[7]

Another facet of his critical conservatism is his unwillingness to abandon the traditional views of the dates and authors of the biblical books without overriding reasons. For example, while Amos is universally regarded as the most uncompromisingly pessimistic of the prophets, his book closes with a promise of salvation. The great majority of the higher critics regard this hopeful conclusion of the last few verses as a later addition by Jewish scribes who were unwilling to permit the words of doom that precede them to close a prophetic book. Buber, by contrast, accepts these verses as an authentic oracle of Amos, and relates them to the development of the messianic hope. In doing so he implies that the critics would do well to let the text revise their image of Amos, instead of eliminating so ancient a passage in order to make the book of Amos conform to their image of the prophet.[8]

The Wellhausen critic generally assumes that a story of an early period which was late in being recorded reflects the outlook of the time of its recording rather than that of the time in which the events purportedly occurred. For instance, if, as appears quite likely to Buber as well as to almost all other critics, the traditions concerning the Patriarchs were not written until around 1,000 B.C., the Wellhausen critic would assume that the stories tell us more about the social and religious conditions of the Palestine of that era than they do of the period around 1,800 B. C. — when the events are supposed to have occurred. Buber, knowing the capacity of men at this stage of civilization for formidable feats of memory directed toward the preservation of ancient traditions — this is still to be observed in the Near East and other areas where written records are not the common thing — maintains that a late literary source, that is, a story which was late in being recorded, may reflect an early religious and social environment. In the case of the materials relating to the Patriarchs, archaeological findings have supported Buber and other critics who shared his point of view. The stories reflect the conditions of an era more than five hundred years earlier than the date at which they were written.[9]

Buber's differences with the Wellhausen scholars are so basic, that he actually has a different view of the way in which the Bible was formed. They thought that various groups in ancient Israel — the historians of the kingdom of Judah, and those of the Northern kingdom, the priests and the prophets — all produced written but somewhat conflicting accounts of the great events of Israel's history. These were thought to have been transmitted to the scribes as sacred documents which could not be destroyed or eliminated, but which the scribes spliced into some semblance of unity. In the process they edited the material into greater conformity with the dogmas of their own day. This would, in the view of the Wellhausen critics, explain both the inconsistencies of prophetic books, such as the one to which we have alluded in connection with Amos, and the literary duplications and repetitions of the Pentateuch.

Buber does not visualize the development of the Bible in these terms. Initially, he sees a process of oral transmission of sacred traditions taking place over many generations. Different groups operated on them — to that extent he is at one with the followers of Wellhausen — but he does not see them as having produced finished and separate literary documents that were later woven together. According to Buber, "What was decisive was what they had in common: each desired to have a share in this common good, this growing Bible, each knowing of it as much as had already taken shape, and taking it openly or covertly as his point of departure." [10]

The compilers, Buber believes, then carried the process further, relating the materials, many of them still in oral form and already manifesting considerable dramatic unity, even more integrally to one another. The perspectives of the different groups produced traditions — he speaks of three, court historians, prophets and priests — whose varying influences are still to be found in the texts. However, their respective roles cannot, as Wellhausen and his followers supposed, be disentangled from one another chapter by chapter, verse by verse, and word by word. Higher criticism cannot reconstruct the different literary strands; the most it can accomplish is to perceive one or another of these traditions as the dominant one in a specific biblical account. For this reason, Buber has called his approach "tradition" criticism and distinguished it from the "source," that is, literary source, criticism of Wellhausen and the rest.[11]

Buber, who believes that all parts of the Jewish Bible were originally intended to be spoken, reveals in his criticism a keen ear for nuances of expression.[12] This has, at times, enabled him to discern connections where other scholars could find only problems calling for the attribution of the materials under consideration to different sources. Most scholars regard the two accounts in which Sarah, Abraham's jealous wife, chases her maid Hagar from the house (Gen 16, and 21:8–21) as different versions of the same incident. They find the stories too repetitious to be, as the Bible clearly represents them, reports of two successive incidents. Because they also find stylistic differences in the two accounts, they assign them to two different literary sources.

Buber draws on the work of Jacob and Cassuto to show that the styles are not as different nor the contents as repetitive as was supposed by the critics who regarded them as the work of different literary sources. Although the work of these two critics provided Buber with valuable insights, it is his own use of the nuances that enables him to show that both accounts properly belong to the cycle of stories about Abraham. Here, we shall note only the parallels he draws between the twenty-first chapter in which Hagar and her son Ishmael are banished for the second time, and the chapter immediately following which deals with the sacrifice of Isaac. There is a deliberate comparison and contrast in the two accounts: Ishmael is sent out to wander in the wilderness; Isaac is led into the wilderness to be bound up. A mother, Hagar, sorrows over Ishmael; a father, Abraham, sorrows over Isaac; God saves Ishmael "from on high" by providing water, He saves Isaac "from on high" (the same phrase is used in both accounts) by providing a ram that will take his place as a sacrifice. Buber concludes that we are dealing with compilers, or more probably with a single one, who had before him materials that may have reflected different traditions, but which, by the time he received them, had become a unified whole whose dramatic potential had not been lost upon him.[13]

Tradition criticism as Buber practices it, also benefits from the fact that his dialogical outlook focuses on the unique aspects of human experience.[14] It precludes an approach to the Bible, or to any other great document in the history of the spirit, which treats it as but one illustration for a general theory of religion. As a result, he is sharply critical of many conclusions to which higher critics were led when they imposed their schemes of religious evolution on the biblical materials.

One major conviction of the Wellhausen critics, based on evolutionary thinking, was that morality was a rather late development of the human race, whereas religious rites were a relatively early phenomenon. For this reason they assumed that the Ten Commandments, as we find them in the twentieth chapter of Exodus and in the fifth chapter of Deuteronomy, are too lofty in moral tone to have originated in as early a period as the Mosaic epoch. In the thirty-fourth chapter of that book they found a series of commandments, also beginning "Thou shalt," which had been delivered in a setting reminiscent of the one connected with the Ten Commandments. The commandments in the thirty-fourth chapter have cultic concerns, such as sacrifices, for their main subject matter. Since the higher critics saw no necessary chronological sequence in the ordering of the chapters, they applied their evolutionary criterion and decided that the Ten Commandments as we know them were a late revision of an original, possibly Mosaic, "cultic decalogue" whose remains we find in the thirty-fourth chapter.

Against this view Buber argues that the commandments

in the thirty-fourth chapter assume a settled agricultural civilization — which the Israelites did not achieve until long after the time of Moses — whereas the Ten Commandments are fit to serve as constituting principles of society, and are therefore appropriate to the Mosaic era when the newly liberated Israelites were being forged into a people. Buber does not believe that this argument proves that Moses was the author of the Ten Commandments; but he does think it shows that they would have been far more relevant to the conditions of life in the Mosaic era than would the "cultic decalogue," which evolutionary assumptions led Wellhausen and some of his followers to propose.[15]

The Wellhausen critic has taught us that the Bible is a human document that reflects the historical conditions of its era. Buber reminds these critics — who have not, on the whole, been very self-conscious about their own assumptions — that they are themselves products of the climate of opinion of the late nineteenth and early twentieth centuries. This is an important point. There can be no possibility of doing justice to the Bible unless we become aware of the point of view we bring to it.

In the last twenty odd years, increased knowledge of the history and culture of the ancient Near East and the abandonment of the more naïve formulations of "religious evolution" have had a sobering effect on Old Testament criticism. While the latest developments confirm many of Buber's specific conclusions, and the generally conservative bent of his approach, they are not attributable to his influence. In recent years a prominent Jewish critic has written an essay on "New Trends in Biblical Criticism," which did not even mention his work.[16] One reason for this neglect is the fact that Buber's studies are suffused with a passionate witness to the biblical faith which, in the eyes of most critics, compromises the "scientific" character of biblical scholarship.

The critics undoubtedly have a point. Witnessing to a faith is not the same sort of activity as the dispassionate analysis of a body of literature. But their case is less persuasive than they think, because history involves far more than dispassionate analysis. In dealing with Moses and figures of similar stature, we confront men who were instrumental in producing new configurations of the human spirit, or, to recall Tillich's distinction, who were bearers of original revelation. Neither the men nor their achievements can be grasped by reducing them to concatenations of psychological, economic, sociological, and other forces which may constitute comfortable points of reference for "scientific" understanding. Buber's approach to the Bible has been fruitful because history, especially when dealing with men and events of such epochal character, requires existential categories of interpretation. This introduces the question of his dialogical reconstruction of the biblical saga which will occupy our attention for the balance of this chapter.

We may best appreciate the point at issue by considering the effective use which H. Richard Niebuhr, a Protestant theologian, makes of Buber's I-Thou and I-It attitudes in formulating his own approach to the understanding of history. In *The Meaning of Revelation* Niebuhr quotes two disparate accounts of the Declaration of Independence. The first is the familiar opening of Lincoln's "Gettysburg Address":

> Four-score and seven years ago our fathers brought forth upon this continent a new nation, conceived in liberty and dedicated to the proposition that all men are created free and equal.

With this he contrasts the account in the *Cambridge Modern History:*

> On July 4, 1776, Congress passed the resolution which made the Colonies independent communities, issuing at the same time the well-known Declaration of Independence. If we regard the Declaration as the assertion of an abstract political theory, criticism and condemnation are easy. It sets out with a general proposition so vague as to be practically useless. The doctrine of the equality of men, unless it be qualified and conditioned by reference to special circumstance, is either a barren truism or a delusion.[17]

Niebuhr observes that there is more at issue between these accounts than the difference in sentiment between the devotion of the patriot and the critical acumen of the "scientific" historian. The terms "Congress" and "our fathers" symbolize two different orders of reality which are reflected in two different types of history. "External" history surveys events from the standpoint of a spectator, as when the historian deals coldly with the Declaration by analyzing its propositional content. Lincoln's "inner" history assumes the viewpoint of the participant and is concerned with the meaning of the Declaration to the people who lived the event; with the dedication to the ideals of freedom and equality that was its heart. Niebuhr concludes: "Moreover it seems evident that the terms the external historian employs are not more truly descriptive of the things-in-themselves than those the statesman uses and that the former's understanding of what really happened is not more accurate than the latter's." [18]

In Buber's biblical studies the distinction has a more limited application, since he finds that all parts of the biblical record are "inner" history. The question that concerns him is the degree of existential involvement which the various texts display. "It is necessary to draw a distinction between saga produced near the historical occurrences, the character of which is enthusiastic report, and saga which is further away from the historical event, and which derives from the tendency to complete and round off what is already given."[19] The primary layers of the sagas are framed in poetry, a form well-suited to preserve them in the memory of the people before they are recorded. In the course of their transmission they are acted upon by the court historians, prophets, and priests so that by the time of their final written compilation they have been considerably recast.

To approach the underlying reality to which the texts bear witness, we must, Buber says, become aware of the traditions that have reworked them and, "Here the procedure of investigation must necessarily be reductive. It must remove layer after layer from the images as set before it, in order to arrive at the earliest of all."[20] This does not give us an objective account of what really happened, but it may enable us to penetrate to the inner core of the Israelites' experience of their history, and to see how they themselves understood the events. However, he warns us that, "We shall not regain a historical nucleus of the saga by eliminating the function of enthusiasm from it."[21]

Buber's account of the crossing of the Red Sea provides a particularly useful illustration of the way his dialogical approach to the Bible influences his critical method, because he uses it as a point of departure for an interpretation of miracle as a form of the encounter between man and the eternal Thou. But before we consider this dialogical interpretation of miracle we should note the kind of critical issue his approach tends to avoid.

Although it would seem to be self-evident, the precise location of the crossing is a matter of considerable concern to the higher critics. They are almost certain that the Israelites did not escape from the Egyptians at that body of water we now call the Red Sea. The Hebrew word *Suf*, traditionally taken as the equivalent of the word later translated as "Red," is actually to be translated as "Reed," and there are still other difficulties connected with the traditional identification of the place of the crossing. In a single sentence, Buber summarizes the most significant hypotheses with which the critics attempt to cope with these difficulties, and he omits all reference to the arguments they use to support them. "We do not know where the pursuers caught up with the fugitives: whether in the neighborhood of the present Suez or, if the Gulf of Suez was then differently shaped from its contemporary form, further north at one of the bitter lakes or the other inner lakes, most probably at the Sirbonian Lake — or even, as some suppose, only at the Gulf of Akaba (though in that case it is hard to understand why the pursuing chariots should not have caught up with them sooner)." [22] He can dismiss these speculations in this cavalier manner because he does not believe that the historical character of the biblical account depends upon our ability to reconstruct details of this kind. The Jewish Bible is historical in the deepest sense, because the great events it reports derive from historical connections and set off fresh historical connections. It is not, like most of the religious epics of other ancient cultures, the record of the lives and loves of the gods in some heavenly locale such as Mount Olympus.[23]

The aspect of the crossing of the sea that absorbs Buber's attention is its importance for our understanding of miracle. As it stands, the biblical account fits beautifully into the supernatural view of miracle as an event which constitutes an utterly inexplicable exception to the normal patterns of natural processes. When Moses divides the seas by stretching his hand across them — creating two walls of raging waters, and a path of dry ground between them through which the Israelites march — any observer would, according to the supernaturalists, be cowed into acknowledging its revelatory significance. The miracle is an "objective" event, whose significance is obvious to all beholders regardless of the attitudes they bring to it.

But this attitude toward miracle is not possible for the man of today. Were he to adopt it, ". . . in deciding to accept the Bible [he] would have to make a sacrifice of intellect which would cut his life irreparably in two, provided he does not want to lapse into the habitual, lazy acceptance of something he does not really believe." [24]

Buber uses his reductive method in an effort to arrive at a dialogical understanding of this great event in the inner history of Israel. He regards the supernatural details as accretions to the original account. The event involved ". . . a natural process or a series of natural processes. . . ." and once again the hypotheses of the critics concerning the precise details are given short shrift, this time by being summarized in a parenthesis, "(whether a combination of tides with unusual winds which raise them tremendously, or the effect of distant volcanic phenomena on the movements of the sea)." [25] These details are not important to Buber; the important thing is that, however it may have come about, the deliverance of the Israelites and the revelatory significance it conveyed to them, constituted a miracle, which, as Buber interprets it, is a special case of the encounter with the eternal Thou. The point is succinctly stated in the following story relating to the Baal Shem Tov, the founder of Hasidism.

> A naturalist came from a great distance to see the Baal Shem and said: "My investigations show that in the course of nature the Red Sea had to divide at the very hour the children of Israel passed through it. Now what about that famous miracle!"
>
> The Baal Shem answered: "Don't you know that God created nature? And He created it so, that at the hour the children of Israel passed through the Red Sea, it had to divide. That is the great and famous miracle!" [26]

It is not supernatural phenomena which constitute the core of the miracle but the abiding sense of astonishment, in which the people experience their deliverence. Subsequent knowledge of a causal character, such as the information brought to the Baal Shem by the scientist, only deepens the people's sense of wonder. "The real miracle means that in the astonishing experience of the event the current system of cause and effect becomes, as it were, transparent and permits a glimpse of the sphere in which a sole power, not restricted by any other, is at work. To live with the miracle means to recognize this power on every given occasion as the effecting one." [27]

Buber is not unlike liberal theologians and higher critics of the Wellhausen type in stripping miracles of their "supernatural accretions," but he differs radically from them in that his dialogical interpretation does not reset the events in a rationalistic framework, which is utterly alien to the biblical outlook. His own "Hasidic" enthusiasm responds to the character of these momentous events, events that are reported in "mythical" terms, and here, he tells us, myth (in contrast to its role in the history of religions where it means stories of the gods and other supernatural beings) means ". . . nothing other than the report by ardent enthusiasts of that which has befallen them." [28]

Buber's position on miracle may be assailed from two sides. Rationalists may protest that all religious enthusiasms spawn myths that elicit devotion from men. By applying Buber's understanding of miracle to the events reported by any sect whatever, we could validate its teachings. Without objective criteria we could not draw distinctions between the inner history of Israel and that of the most superstitious and barbaric cults. Once again Buber would answer that our yearning for certainty cannot alter the character of reality. There are many reasons why men of sense and of sensitivity would reject fanatical cults, but they are neither objective nor demonstrable.

On the other hand, supernaturalists among the Orthodox parties of Judaism and Christianity might deride Buber's dialogical interpretation of miracles because of its emphasis on the inner attitude of the participants. They could claim that he locates the miracle within the person experiencing it, rather than in the world "out there." But Buber does not locate them within man; like all revelations, of which they are a special case, they are the product of an encounter between God and man.

In any event, the supernaturalists fail to see that their literal acceptance of the biblical accounts involves the Bible itself in psychological absurdities. It is conceivable that, centuries after a wonder like that involved in Moses' dividing of the waters, the people forgot the miracle and turned away from the God who wrought it. But in the biblical account of the Exodus from Egypt and the wandering in the desert, which the supernaturalists urge us to accept in its literal form, the people turn away from God and His servant Moses almost immediately after He has performed such awful and, ostensibly, objective wonders. In contrast with the literalism of the supernaturalists, Buber's dialogical interpretation of miracle is selective as to detail, but it captures the existential significance of the event and sets it meaningfully within the rhythm of the Mosaic saga — the continual rebelliousness of the people and their subsequent turning to God.

Out of the depths of a life rich in dialogue Buber has etched a credo of biblical, and religious, authenticity, ". . . *what happened once happens now and always, and the fact of its happening to us is a guarantee of its having happened.*" [29] This does not mean that events repeat themselves. "That which exists is unique," says Buber, "and it happens but once." [30] But the conditions, the natural processes which form an integral aspect of the environment in which they take place, are the same throughout the generations. Buber cannot accept the assumption of Jewish Orthodoxy that God's relations with Israel were "supernatural" until the end of the period of prophecy, some four hundred years before the Christian Era, and that since that time He no longer addresses men "face to face." The events of the biblical epoch were, as the occasions of original revelation, of momentous significance; but the men involved in them were still men, living under the conditions of existence as we know them.

Readers familiar with contemporary theological trends find striking similarities between Buber's approach to the Bible and that of the New Orthodoxy which is so prominent in Protestant circles. Thinkers who share this point of view stress the sense of the living God, and many other teachings of Christian Orthodoxy — original sin, the divine aspect of the two natures of Jesus Christ, the Trinity, the resurrection of the dead — which had been vitiated by the rationalistic tendencies of liberal theology. On the other hand, the term "New" indicates their realization that there can be no return to a pre-scientific world-view that conceives of a "three-story" universe in which heaven and hell are spatially located above and below the earth, whose normal routines are subject to arbitrary incursions from the powers that inhabit the other realms.

Whatever points he may hold in common with various representatives of the New Orthodoxy, Buber's approach does not reflect a commitment to the dogmatic formulations of any religious tradition. In a rare departure into a "confessional" mode of address, he has written:

> . . . my own belief in revelation, which is not mixed up with any "orthodoxy," does not mean that I believe that finished statements about God were handed down from heaven to earth. Rather it means that the human substance is melted by the spiritual fire which visits it, and there now breaks forth from it a word, a statement, which is human in its meaning and form, human conception and human speech, and yet witnesses to Him who stimulated it and to His will.[31]

The vehicle of revelation, the prophet, whose entire being serves as the "mouth of God," responds to the God he encounters in an I-Thou relation, and then converts the message into speech. "Before the word is spoken by him in human language it is spoken to him in another language, from which he has to translate it into human language, to him this word is spoken as between person and person." [32] Hosea is impelled, through encounter with the living God, to marry a prostitute who persists in her promiscuity; and he comes to see his relations with this woman as an image of God's relations with faithless Israel. Jeremiah is impelled to go to the house of a potter, watching in fascination as the potter rolls the clay upon his wheel. The first vessel produced is spoiled and the potter reworks it into another one; and Jeremiah comes to see the process as an image of God's struggle to rework intractable Israel into a holy nation.

The prophets and other recipients of divine revelation are not passive recording instruments of mysterious words from "above." "The man . . . who is the 'mouth' of the revelation, is indeed this, not a speaking-tube or any kind of instrument, but an organ, which sounds according to its own laws; and to sound means to *modify*." [33] Although men certainly modify the message according to the finite character of their own nature, that is, according to limitations imposed upon them by their personal attributes and by the cultural setting in which they live, biblical revelation is not to be understood in purely human terms as the product of "religious geniuses." "It is not man's own power that works here, nor is it God's pure effective passage, but it is a mixture of the divine and the human." [34] But there is no possibility of objectively measuring the extent of the divine and human elements involved in any given revelatory utterance. We may recall Buber's view that, when reading the Bible, we must respond to that which we are led, by concentrating our whole beings on it, to regard as willed by God for us.[35] This means that the man of faith must always live in "holy insecurity"; faith must encompass and not expunge doubt.[36]

Since Buber's understanding of faith is expressed in large measure in terms of "the prophetic faith," an objection to his position may well be made on the grounds that the prophets, in the declaration "Thus saith the Lord," which preceded so many of their oracles, made no qualifying remarks regarding personal contributions of their own which adulterated the purity of the divine word. It is obvious that qualifications of this kind are products of the sophisticated outlook of the man of today. In support of Buber's position, however, we ought to note that in the biblical record itself there are suggestions that, for prophet and hearer alike, the word of God was not a simple matter of conviction and declaration reflecting a state of certainty as to the fundamental questions confronting Israel.

That the phenomenon of prophecy was not unproblematical for the Israelites is indicated by the two criteria for determining the false prophet given in the book of Deuteronomy. One of them, to be found in 18:22, states that a false prophet is one whose words are not fulfilled; the other, which supplements it, is stated in 13:1–5, and holds that even a man whose words are fulfilled is a false prophet if he summons the people to follow other gods. In the book of Jeremiah — the only one that provides us with considerable biographical details of a prophetic career — we have an incident (recorded in the twenty-seventh and twenty-eighth chapters) that sheds considerable light on the issue of whether the prophet himself was capable of tolerating existential doubt.

At a time when Judah and neighboring kingdoms were conspiring against the Babylonian power, God commanded Jeremiah to set a yoke of wood upon his neck and to parade through the streets of Jerusalem with it, in order to convey the message that all conspiracies against Babylon must fail, and that the conspiring kingdoms would fall under its yoke. When Jeremiah fulfilled the divine will, he was accosted by another prophet, Hananiah, who removed the yoke from his shoulders, broke it before the people, and proclaimed — in the name of the Lord of Hosts, the God of Israel — that within two years Babylon's power would similarly be broken.

What were the leaders of Israel to do? Were they to continue their plans or not? With the perspective of history we know that Jeremiah was right; but they had no such perspective. Furthermore, Jeremiah himself was shaken. If the general impression of the prophet as a man with absolute certainty in his possession of God's truth were a valid one, he should have immediately denounced Hananiah and called upon God to pour his wrath upon the head of the imposter. Instead, he replied: "Amen! the Lord do so!" (28:6). He departed after warning his hearers that the true prophets of former days did not speak comforting words which the people wanted to hear and that, since Hananiah was doing just that, the burden of proof was upon him.

Later Jeremiah received another word which convinced him that Hananiah was wrong. Denouncing Hananiah as a false prophet, he substituted a yoke of iron for the wooden one which had been broken by Hananiah, thereby reiterating the original message in even stronger terms. But in the immediate situation, when Hananiah broke the wooden yoke and confronted him with a word that contradicted his own, he went on his way. The fact that the prophets prefaced their messages by saying "Thus saith the Lord" conveys their confidence and certainty regarding the truth of their message, but the mere fact that Jeremiah could conceive of another prophet having a contradictory, and *valid* word of the Lord, shows that his certainty was not absolute.[37]

In Buber's view no supernatural phenomena validate the claims to divine origin made on behalf of any revelatory message, and no special gifts exempt the prophets from the limitations of human finitude. All men stand in a situation of faith before the ultimate, and in competition with the crowd-pleasing performances of the "Hananiahs" the true word is often powerless. "God does not corroborate it; He leaves to man the choice of opening his heart to the hard truth or of accepting the easy fraud as truth; He does not in any way lighten this choice for man; He does not throw onto the scales of man's soul even a particle of His limitless power." [38]

If we grant the validity of Buber's understanding of the Bible as a record of dialogical encounters between man and God, we may wonder how the man of today is to bridge the gap that separates him from the immediacies of encounters which took place in ages long past. In this connection, we may recall Tillich's distinction between original and dependent revelation.[39] The original events break new ground, but subsequent generations may appropriate their significance by existentially relating to them, as Lincoln appropriated the significance of the Declaration of Independence. "The Jewish Bible," says Buber, in making this point, "is the historical record of a world swinging between creation and redemption, which, in the course of its history, experiences revelation, a revelation which *I* experience *if I am there.*" [40]

Kierkegaard made this appropriation a central point of his approach to Christian truth. He spoke of the "man of today," that is, of his day, as a "disciple at second hand" who, in reading the Gospel accounts of the life and death of Jesus of Nazareth, was at no disadvantage in comparison with the "disciples at first hand" who were actually present at those events. The fact that Jesus was the God-man, which for Kierkegaard represented the heart of the Christian message, is not something that could be witnessed with the "naked eye." Thousands saw him without realizing this central truth about him, and his own disciples lost faith at the crucifixion. Therefore, any man of today who appropriates the meaning existentially — by recognizing Jesus as the God-man, and incorporating the significance of this paradox in his life — stands closer to the meaning of the events of Jesus' life than did those who actually saw them without realizing their significance.[41]

The notion that faith involves existential appropriation of the meaning of revelation is not alien to the Jewish tradition. The Passover Holiday, which commemorates the Exodus from Egpyt, is saturated with it. In every home a sacred meal, the Seder, is held to inaugurate the festivities. As a part of them the Passover Haggadah, which contains the story of the Exodus and related material, is chanted by the assembled family. The Rabbis who compiled the Haggadah continually urge the individual Jew to celebrate the Passover by reliving the event of the Exodus as though he were himself being freed from slavery in Egypt. In the section in which the point is stressed most emphatically, they refer to a verse of the Jewish Bible as the source of this idea:

> In every generation it is each man's duty to look upon himself as if he personally had come out of Egypt. For we are commanded: "Tell your son in that day that it is because of what the Lord did for *me* when I came out of Egypt." [Exod (13:8)] It was not only our forefathers whom God saved; He saved us too.[42]

The faith of Israel is rooted in the personal appropriation of the inner meaning of the great events of her history, of the Exodus, Sinai, and the rest. If one asks why these events and not others, or why the biblical record rather than the Platonic literature should be determinative for the faith of the man of today — who is the product of so many other historical influences and is shaped by so many other literatures — the answer lies in the arbitrariness of history. It was the events recorded in the Bible and these alone that molded the faith of Israel. Therefore, to the extent that a man of today becomes a Jew or a Christian, these events become determinative for his personal faith.

At Passover every family in Israel celebrating the Exodus becomes a bearer of the revelation that was embodied in the event — at least to the extent that individual members of the family appropriate its significance. As long as the memory of the event is preserved, Buber believes that appropriation is always possible. "We Jews are a community based on memory. A common memory has kept us together and enabled us to survive." [43] In the Seder, he finds the most striking evidence of the passion to hand down traditions which has preserved this common memory.

Handing down traditions may become an automatic affair which is repetitious and sterile, but it need not be so. "For tradition does not consist in letting contents and forms pass on, finished and inflexible, from generation to generation . . . a generation can only receive the teachings in the sense that it renews them." [44] Hasidism understood this very well, and this is one source of the vitality of its teachings.

> When Rabbi Noah, Rabbi Mordecai's son, assumed the succession [as leader of a local Hasidic community] after his father's death, his disciples noticed that there were a number of ways in which he conducted himself differently from his father, and asked him about this.

> "I do just as my father did," he replied. "He did not imitate, and I do not imitate." [45]

Yet the new generation must not, in the name of appropriating the faith, be casual in dealing with the words of the original revelation. It must know that it confronts something holy. Buber, who speaks of reforging the tradition in the fire of his personal relation to the absolute, does so with reverence for the words of the Bible. Words such as "Israel" and "Messiah" acquire a special aura because they have borne the mission of the people through the centuries, and the sacrifices that the people have made in responding to them have continually increased their power. It was with this point in mind that a Hasidic master initiated an exchange with a group of his disciples:

> "When you utter a word before God, then enter into that word with every one of your limbs."
>
> One of his listeners asked: "How can a big human being possibly enter into a little word?"
>
> "Anyone who thinks himself bigger than the word," [he answered] "is not the kind of person we are talking about." [46]

By entering into the word with every one of his limbs, that is, by bringing the sum total of his life's experience to the reading of the Bible and holding himself open to the possibility of fresh response, the man of today may encounter the revelatory significance embodied in the texts. But there can be no guarantee; he may fail to encounter the meaning altogether, or a text that stirs him deeply on one occasion may leave him dry on another.

> . . . the Word of God crosses my vision like a falling star to whose fire the meteorite will bear

> witness without making it light up for me, and I myself can only bear witness to the light but not produce the stone and say "This is it." [47]

The man who appropriates the revelatory significance of the Bible is confronted by the God of relation. The view of God that dominates the biblical accounts is not that of an almighty magician moving people around as though they were pieces on a chessboard, but of a God who operates within limits He imposes upon Himself. He seeks to bring forth a creature, man, who will enter into dialogue with Him. "And if He was not a person in Himself, He, so to speak, [this is the way it is experienced in the encounter of faith] became one in creating man, in order to love man and be loved by him — in order to love me and be loved by me." [48]

Man as the creature wooed by God, this is the overriding image that lends the biblical saga its poignancy. God does not coerce intractable man: "He who rejects Him is not struck by lightning; he who elects Him does not find hidden treasures." [49] Although some sections of the Bible contradict this assertion, as when Korach and other rebels against the leadership of Moses are swallowed into the earth (we must remember the highly selective character of Buber's reading), the books of Jeremiah and Job and many of the Psalms testify to the agony of those who saw the wicked prosper and the righteous suffer. God does not override the human will. He wants to work with and through it.

As Buber sees it, the biblical saga is unified by the messianic hope which emerges out of Israel's persistent failure to fulfill the will of God.

The Bible begins with the words, "In the beginning," but Buber finds a series of beginnings — with Adam, with Noah, and with Abraham.[50] The first race of man covers the earth with violence, and God destroys it with the flood. The second race begins with the sons of Noah, the man "righteous in his generation," who was saved from the flood; and this race is no better than the first. It builds the Tower of Babel in defiance of God, who, having promised Noah that he would never again destroy man, scatters the people into many lands and divides them by means of many languages, thereby setting the stage of history as we know it. It also sets the stage for a third beginning.

Since men are now divided geographically and culturally, there is no longer a possibility of bringing them, as a unified race in conformity with God's will, into that genuine community which God intended in creating man. "In order that the multiplicity of people may become one people of peoples, they must," says Buber, "first be shown what a real people, a unity made up of the various many, is like." [51]

The call of Abraham — his being summoned to leave his natural setting in the house and country of his father to go to a country that God will show him — is the new beginning which is also the beginning of the mission of Israel. The descendents of Abraham, the Hebrews, are to show mankind the way to its true humanity, by establishing a nation grounded in peace and justice. The call of Abraham represents the beginning, but the venture is not formally inaugurated with the people, as a people, until the newly liberated Israelites gather at Mount Sinai.

At Mount Sinai God enters into a covenant with Israel. The covenant has often been misinterpreted by being thought of in contractual terms, but it is more like a marriage vow linking God and Israel in a relation of mutual trust. He promises them His special guidance, and they promise Him obedience. This covenant is the basis of the idea of "The Chosen People," for God said, "Now therefore, if ye will hearken to my voice indeed, and keep my covenant then ye shall be mine own treasure from among all peoples. . . ." (Exod 19:5). Only if they listen to God and obey, will they become that which He intends them to be: a holy people which will point the way to true humanity to all mankind. To do this they must allow God's will to determine the entire substance of the national life. Thus, Moses may be regarded as the inaugurator of what Buber has called the "religious realism" peculiar to Israel:

> . . . which has no room for a truth remaining abstract, hovering self-sufficiently above reality, but for which every truth is bound up with a demand which man, the people, Israel are called upon to fulfill integrally on earth. Now integral fulfillment means two things: it must, in the first place, comprise the whole life, the whole civilization of a people, economy, society, and state, and secondly, it must incorporate the whole of the individual, his emotions and his will, his actions and abstentions, his life at home and in the market place, in the temple and in the popular assembly.[52]

In effect, Moses instituted a "theo-political" principle as the one by which Israel was to order her life. Buber uses this term in order to distinguish it from "theocracy," another term which means the rule of God. But in theocracies there was a fixed way of choosing leaders. In some, an elaborate procedure was involved in qualifying for the priesthood, and selecting rulers from among the priests involved another elaborate procedure. The rule instituted by Moses was a more direct form of the rule of God. Here, God's earthly representatives were charismatic leaders, that is, their only claim to authority was the fact that they had been seized by the divine spirit.[53]

In the time of the Judges, Israel was tested to see whether she could live in accordance with this theo-political principle. The Judges were not rulers in any earthly sense, but were men from one or another of the tribes of Israel who, when the divine spirit was upon them, led the people through a crisis, and then retired to their homes. But the people failed the test. They found the burden of being directly ruled by God, which in human terms meant being ruled only on a sporadic basis, too great to bear. They were unsuccessful in war and lawless in their relations with one another, and the book of Judges closes with an epitaph for the theo-political experiment: "In those days there was no king in Israel; every man did that which was right in his own eyes" (Judges 21:25).

The people rejected the direct rule of God and called for an earthly king. "The people call for security from above against death and interregnum, and for a succession which would not suffer interruption with its consequent dangers; they call for hereditary heavenly favor like 'all the nations' have." The roots of messianism are to be found in this critical juncture in the history of Israel. For the king is the "messiah," which is simply an English transliteration of the Hebrew word that means the "anointed one." The king was anointed with oil, a preservative, because he was supposed to preserve the covenantal relation between God and Israel.[54]

Yet, the more the kings succeeded in worldly terms — by bringing the people a measure of security and prosperity — the more they failed from the standpoint of faith. Instead of preserving the covenantal relation with God, they either led the people astray, or did nothing to prevent their falling away from God.

One offense against the covenant was that the kings themselves led the people into alliances with other nations, which, in those days, involved recognition of the gods of those nations as well. But the major offenses were prevalent among the people themselves. As they became prosperous they became absorbed with agriculture and with the Baalim, the gods of the pagan fertility cults. The Israelites worshipped these gods in the customary way, by having sexual intercourse with the temple prostitutes who were an official part of the fertility cults. They hoped, by performing an act integrally related to the process of human fertility, to induce the Baalim to bring about the fertility of their soil.

The people carried their faithlessness even further. They treated the God of Israel, Creator of heaven and earth, as though He were nothing more than an idol. They oppressed their fellow men and sought to bribe God with sacrifices — forgetting that their God demanded justice and righteousness before sacrifice. They forgot that their God was concerned with the heart, with motivation, and that any sacrifice that was not motivated by the intention to bring the entire self into conformity with His moral purpose, was an abomination in His eyes.[55]

In protesting against these abuses the prophets emerged as witnesses to His will. "At no other time or place," says Buber, "has the spirit been served in the human world with such militancy, generation after generation, as it was by the prophets of Israel." [56] But he sees the prophetic protest as the beginning of a new pattern in the history of the faith of Israel. From Moses through Samuel (the last of the

Judges) the power to rule and the role of witness were united in one man. Now they were split. The king was the man of power who opposed the spirit, and the prophet, the servant of the spirit, was without power. Again and again, the prophets risked persecution — and suffered it — in their efforts to recall the kings to a sense of their covenantal responsibilities, but with little or no success.[57] "The history of the kings is," in Buber's view, "the history of the failure of him who has been anointed to realize the promise of his anointing." [58]

The experience of generations of faithless kings produced a darkening of the prophetic vision. "The rebelliousness of the hour, rebelling against the prophetic teaching, directs the heart of the prophet to the future, which will fulfill his teaching." [59] Against the faithless kings they knew, the prophets set the image of the "true anointed one," the Messiah, who would do just what the many kings failed to do, who would establish peace by ruling justly.[60] The messianic vision was a message of hope, but Buber never lets us forget that it was born in bitter disappointment.

The subsequent history of messianism, including its reaching out to the nations in the person of Jesus of Nazareth, whom they hailed as the *Christos* (Greek for Messiah) is only to be understood against this background of the opposition of king and prophet, of power and the spirit.

The fall of Jerusalem in 586 B.C. and the exile of the people to Babylon, fulfilled the warnings of the prophets. A short time after this catastrophe, around 540 B.C., a new stage in the history of Israel's faith begins. It is inaugurated by a prophet who brings a message of hope: the Babylonian kingdom is about to fall and Israelites are to return to their country. But even these glad tidings witness to the deepening cleavage between the sources of power and the witness of the spirit. The restoration to Palestine will not be effected by a member of the Davidic line, but by a pagan king, Cyrus the Mede.[61] And the prophet who announces the event does not even step forward into history, but remains shrouded in anonymity in the book of Isaiah, whose disciple he was.[62]

The higher critics have unanimously concluded that we hear a new prophetic voice from (at least) the fortieth chapter on, because the original Isaiah began his ministry some two centuries before the period of Babylon's fall and because there is a marked stylistic difference between those chapters and the earlier ones. Therefore, they have spoken of this anonymous prophet as Deutero-Isaiah (deutero is the Greek word for "second"). Some critics have divided the book further by speaking of a Third Isaiah whose work they purport to find in chapters 56–66, and some have even found a number of other distinct prophetic sources. Buber claims that almost all of chapters 40–55 are the work of Deutero-Isaiah and that only a few passages in the rest of the book are from his hand.[63]

The message of Deutero-Isaiah is the most mysterious one in the Jewish Bible. At its heart stands the reaffirmation of Israel's mission; she is to bring the light of the Lord to the nations. But this joyful proclamation is encased in a darker view of history than that held by any of Deutero-Isaiah's predecessors among the prophets. It is not a king of Israel who is to be the Messiah; the time has passed when the prophet can hope that the Davidic line will, should it again assume power, fulfill the purpose of the anointing. In the oracles of Second Isaiah the hope of Israel has shifted from the monarchy to the Suffering Servant of the Lord.[64]

The identity of the Servant * has been a baffling problem for the commentators. Because he suffers a vicarious death for the sins of many — being led like a lamb to the slaughter — Christianity has identified him with Jesus. But this flies in the face of the fact that Israel itself is called the Servant in a number of verses. The identification with the people Israel is also problematical since an individual is clearly represented in some of the poems. Buber tries to overcome the difficulty by regarding the Servant as a "prophetic core" which stands for the people and which will one day accomplish its mission. In his view, the poems at times refer to the sequence of prophets as a collective representation of Israel, and at times they allude to the career and sufferings of individual prophets.[66]

He finds three stages of development in the prophet's messianic vision: the call, and with it a readiness for suffering; the actual suffering; and the final one, the emergence of the messianic leader out of the Servant who has been purified by suffering.[67] Buber supposes that the prophet himself may not have been clear as to the way the message would finally work itself out in history, ". . . it was laid upon the anonymous prophet to announce a mystery, not to interpret it." Nor is he certain of the extent to which the prophet regarded himself as a figure of messianic potential. Some of the passages connected with the Servant suggest that Deutero-Isaiah saw himself as a link in a chain of figures that would finally culminate in a Messiah who would be a prophet rather than a king.[68]

Because false messiahs have appeared so often in Jewish

* The poems in which he appears are but a fragment of the total work of the Second Isaiah; according to Buber they are: 43:1–9; 49:1–9a; 50:4–9 and 52:13–53:12.[65]

history and caused the people a great deal of suffering, Buber is deeply suspicious of any man who would identify himself as the Messiah. Jewish history has taught him that apart from everything else, the publicity attendant on messianic claims, at least until modern times, was enough in itself to provide a temptation that would be too great to be overcome by the type of person inclined to make such a claim.[69] He finds the high-water mark of biblical messianism in the prophecies of the Second Isaiah, because anonymity is a central feature of the vision. Through the years Buber has been all but haunted by the verse in which the Servant declares, ". . . He hath made my mouth like a sharp sword, in the shadow of His hand hath He hid me; and He hath made me a polished shaft, in His quiver hath He concealed me" (49:2). In this declaration Buber sees a check on pretenders, for, "The arrow in the quiver is not its own master; the moment at which is shall be drawn out is not for it to determine." [70]

The next stage in the development of messianism presents such a radical deepening of the split between power and the spirit that Buber regards it as a retrogression from the historical realism that was one of the great glories of prophetic religion. It comes at a time in Jewish history, around the first half of the second century, before the Christian era, when persecution and bloodshed were so rampant—as they were to remain right through the second century A.D.—that "people tend then not merely to despair of the saving achievement of the king, but of that of earthly man in general. The world can no longer be redeemed by the world." [71] This ultimate pessimism about the world and history gave rise to a new form of literature, apocalypse (from the Greek "to uncover," hence "reveal").

Apocalypse is a literary form as well as a way of thinking. As found in the book of Daniel, the one example of it in the Jewish Bible; in the book of Revelation, which concludes the New Testament; and in so many of the works of the "Inter-Testamental" literature, composed in the course of the long time of trouble and not included in either Testament — it reflected the influence of Persian religion. This religion was thoroughly dualistic, dividing the world between the god of good and the god of evil. These gods commanded enormous hosts of angels and demons and were engaged in continual warfare, using the earth and the souls of the men upon it as the crucial battleground. As the pressures of persecution and bloodshed sapped the strength of the Jewish hope for a redemption that would occur in the midst of history, they evoked an increasing concern with eschatology, the study of "last things," that is, of the catastrophic end of history. To this interest, the riot of fantastic imagery that permeated Persian religion was peculiarly appropriate.

Since the apocalyptic books dealt with the hideous doom that God would ultimately wreak on the enemies of the faithful, it was important that they be understood only by those for whom they were intended. Therefore, the occupying powers, such as the Romans, were represented by means of still more fantastic imagery: monsters with the body of one animal, the wings of some great bird, and one or more heads from still other beasts.

Another device used by apocalyptic writers to obscure the historical references contained in their works was to attribute their composition to an author of some previous epoch — Enoch, Baruch, and Ezra were used more than once — and to provide a historical setting that was purportedly that of the time of the pseudonymous author. Thus higher critics, including Buber, argue that the book of Daniel, directed against persecutions of the Syrian king Antiochus Epiphanes around 170–164 B.C., was, for this reason, set in Babylon at the time of the fall of that kingdom to Cyrus.

Buber, in contrasting apocalypse with prophecy, claims that, while the prophet spoke his message directly to an audience (unless he was forcibly prevented from doing so), the apocalyptic authors were writers who lacked all sense of immediacy and wrote reflectively for their notebooks.[72] This characterization may be appropriate to some apocalyptic writings, but for the most part, it is unfair. The apocalyptic authors had an audience very much in mind, and they directed a message of hope to it. But this message contrasts sharply with that of the prophets, and Buber's analysis of their respective approaches to history points up the differences between them.

The prophet speaks to the people in terms of the concrete immediacies of an historical situation. Isaiah tells Ahaz not to seek an alliance with Assyria; Jeremiah warns Zedekiah not to form alliances against Babylon. All of them warn the people that if they do not desist from social injustice and false worship they will be destroyed, but the instruments of destruction with which they threaten the people are earthly, historically identifiable empires. The entire drama is enacted within the confines of history and it is acted out by men whose freedom enables them to make responsible decisions within it. Buber insists that the prophets, ". . . do not warn against something which will happen in any case, but against that which will happen if those who are called upon to turn [to God] do not." [73]

Apocalyptic literature knows nothing of freedom. It does not call upon sinners to turn but promises the persecuted faithful a vindication at the end of time, namely, a violent cataclysm that will end the world and mark the inauguration of eternal bliss for them and of eternal torture for their enemies. This is the hope conveyed by apocalyptic literature. And the apocalyptic writers were certain that their predictions would be fulfilled. "Everything here," says Buber, "is predetermined, all human decisions are only sham struggles. The future does not come to pass; the future is already present in heaven, as it were, present from the beginning. Therefore, it can be 'disclosed' to the speaker and he can disclose it to others." [74]

The record is fixed, like a film strip that has only to be projected. There is no possibility of sinners turning, nor is there any possibility of righteousness influencing the historical order. The one thing the faithful can do in the effort to overcome their utter passivity is to try to determine, from clues in the Sacred Scriptures, just when it is that the appointed end, so ardently longed for, is to come. The book of Daniel provides an excellent example of this when it interprets Jeremiah's prophecy of redemption from exile after seventy years as weeks of years (four hundred and ninety years), thereby converting it into a promise of redemption from the oppression the Jews were experiencing at the time the book of Daniel was written.

Ironically, when most people speak of prophecy they have apocalypse in mind; they think of the apocalyptic plumbing of the secrets of the predetermined divine plan, and of the fantastic imagery which the apocalyptic writers associate with the vindication of the righteous and the destruction of the wicked. Nothing could be more mistaken. Apocalypse, which deals with a God so utterly remote from man that no contact between them is possible (it is angels who bring men the secrets of the "hidden things") and so powerful that no freedom of human response is conceivable, stands at the opposite pole from prophecy, which emphasized direct encounter between God and man.

The differences between prophecy and apocalypse extend to their messianism. The original prophetic hope for an ideal king was certainly this-worldly, and even the messianism of Deutero-Isaiah, with its more pessimistic outlook does not retreat from history. "Deutero-Isaiah certainly does not think of the final, fulfilling appearance of the servant of God as one which has been sent down from heaven to earth. This changes with . . . the book of Daniel. The 'one like to a man,' the eschatological representative of Israel, is conveyed 'with the clouds of heaven' before the throne of God." [75] In shifting our attention from the prophecy of Deutero-Isaiah to the apocalyptic thinking of the book of Daniel we move from the domain of a faith rooted in history to one rooted in supernatural fantasies. The prophetic vision of the Messiah was one of human fulfillment, the apocalyptic one is that of a supernatural Savior sent from above.

When the Jewish people were driven into exile, their Messiah had not come. But the hope never vanished. Buber finds the exiled people in a state of continual tension between the prophetic and the apocalyptic versions of the messianic longing. In Hasidism, more than in any other aspect of the tradition, he finds a realization, and even an amplification, of prophetic messianism.[76]

> The Hasidic message of redemption should be understood in connection with the attitude of the Baal Shem to redemption. It rises against the messianic self-differentiation between one man and other men, between one age and other ages, be-

tween one act and other acts. To the whole of mankind is given the power to cooperate, all ages stand immediately face to face with redemption, all action for God's sake may be called messianic action.[77]

5. Hasidism: The Hallowing of the Everyday

> He shall seize the quality of eagerness with might, he shall rise eagerly from sleep, for he is become hallowed, and is become another man, and is worthy to beget, and is become imbued with the quality of the Holy One, praised be He, who begat worlds.[1]

Martin Buber tells us that, when he came upon this sublime world-affirming description of the man of genuine piety, the words flashed toward him and converted him into a disciple of the religious leader who uttered them. The leader was the Baal Shem Tov, the founder of Hasidism, and the love of the world expressed in this saying has impressed many Jews since the Baal Shem first spoke them in the middle of the eighteenth century. Yet, though Hasidism swept rapidly through the Jewish villages of Poland and the rest of Eastern Europe, it never penetrated the more sophisticated elements of European Jewry, because it failed to break out of the essentially medieval frame of reference that had, from its beginnings, characterized its outlook.

At the turn of this century, the cultivated Jews in Western and Central Europe — long since liberated from the cultural and social restrictions of ghetto life — were prone to regard the Hasidim * with the distaste that most high church

* The Hebrew plural for *Hasid* is *Hasidim*, "the pious ones."

Episcopalians today direct toward the members of Jehovah's Witnesses. For the Hasidim clung to all sorts of superstitious beliefs and magical practices, not the least of which was their idolatrous regard for the Zaddikim * (literally, "the Righteous Ones"), who were hereditary leaders of the local groups into which the movement had quickly fragmented.

Since Buber had, by the time of his rapturous discovery of the teaching quoted above, established himself among the intelligentsia of Central Europe, his deep interest in the teachings of this reactionary movement must have baffled many of his contemporaries. Buber himself was aware of the anomalous character of his involvement with this movement, for in one of his very rare excursions into autobiography, he wrote an essay dealing with his way to Hasidism. We have already given the essential details of the story: the immersion in European culture that resulted in estrangement from Judaism; the engagement with Zionism that produced a thirst for Jewish learning; and the encounter with the fervent faith of the Baal Shem that led to his absorption with the teachings of Hasidism for five years, from 1904 to 1909.[2]

During those five years of intensive study, Buber began his life-long work of shaping, retelling, and interpreting the chaotic literary materials of Hasidism. In 1957 he described this work as a form of stewardship, a drive to bring the message of this self-encapsulated sect to a world that so desperately needed to hear it.[3]

The results of this stewardship have been astonishing. At the time he began his work Hasidism was unknown to much of the world and scorned by cultured Jews, but it is rapidly

* The singular is Zaddik.

becoming a part of our cultural heritage. This is still more astonishing when one realizes that even today the Hasidim resolutely ignore the social and cultural concerns of the modern world. Yet the current surge of interest in their teachings is not based on antiquarianism — it represents a search for meaning, for the force that quickened the early years of its creative power, roughly from 1750 to 1825, as these years have been brought before the world by the work of Martin Buber.

There is no doubt that Buber's reading of Hasidism is highly selective. His primary concern has been to convey the power and profundity of the best elements of the movement and not to present a balanced historical study of its development. Furthermore, no one who has read his philosophical works, especially *I and Thou,* can doubt that, in Buber, Hasidism has found an interpreter who is anything but passive. As its light streamed upon him he refracted it with his own peculiar intensity. He has given Hasidism a clarity and a unified thrust which no movement — spread over so wide an area, over so long a period of time, and lacking all semblance of institutional discipline — could actually possess. In addition, he has emphasized and adapted those aspects of its teachings that bear most directly on our contemporary problems.

The omissions and more peculiar personal colorations that characterize Buber's treatment of Hasidism will doubtless be brought to our attention by other workers in the field — to some extent they already have been.[4] But no amount of critical research will erase the image of the movement that emerges from his work, because that image, which penetrates to its deepest significance, is vitally relevant to us.

Buber finds no radical departure from the patterns of

Jewish life and teaching in Hasidism; in it he finds a concentration of all the creative factors of the tradition. Its teachings resemble those of many other Jewish movements.[5] Its strictures against formalized worship devoid of the inner attitude of devotion recall the Prophets, while some of the tales extolling the virtues and power of the Zaddikim are prefigured in stories about the great Rabbis of earlier epochs. But many readers of Buber's various collections of Hasidic materials will be struck most forcefully by the affinities between Hasidism and the New Testament teachings. In the course of studying Buber's interpretation of Hasidism we shall have occasion to observe some of these affinities, but it should be noted at the outset that there can be no question of direct influence. The Hasidim, as Jews of a most rigorous exclusiveness, would never have studied the texts or teachings of Christianity, because they regarded any contact with alien religions as sinful.[6]

When we consider Buber's account of the historical circumstances out of which Hasidism developed, we find that although the movement was thoroughly and traditionally Jewish, it attained its peculiar mode of expression by reacting forcefully against many of the worst features of the Judaism of its day. Some of these were tendencies of long standing while others were the products of the turbulent century that preceded the emergence of this movement.

In 1648, Polish Jewry was rocked by the first of a series of savage massacres that persisted for more than a decade and shattered its foundations. Until the time of the Nazis, they constituted as terrible a persecution as Judiasm had encountered in its dispersion through the world. The extent of their savagery is indicated by reports that the Cossacks raped Jewish women, and then sewed live cats into their abdomens.

Thousands were killed and many thousands more were left homeless. The terror and the refugees were a combination that completely disrupted life in the surviving Jewish communities of Eastern Europe.

The longing for the Messiah, which is an integral part of Judaism, is normally kept in check by the sobriety of its tradition of learning and the discipline imposed by adherence to the Mosaic laws. But in terrifying circumstances of this kind the Jewish people became susceptible to fantastic extremes of messianic fervor. The Jews of Poland responded in vast numbers to the messianic pretensions of one Sabbatai Zevi, whose main claim to the office, if we may trust the judgment of the most highly regarded chronicler of the movement, was the personal magnetism that he, a manic-depressive, exerted in his moments of exaltation. But his movement derived its potency from the fact that Nathan of Gaza, a mystic who had some stature as a thinker and considerable talent as a propogandist, became its guiding genius. The influence of this movement was not limited to the Jews of Poland; other Jewish communities in Europe also responded to it and, in that same decade, the 1660's, there was a great deal of messianic agitation in the Christian community as well. All this may indicate that the apocalyptic spirit was "in the air," but that is outside the scope of our study. The fact is that the claim of Sabbatai Zevi was made at a time when the Jews of Poland were longing, as never before, for a supernatural deliverer from the living hell that their earthly life had become.

In 1667, when the expectations of world Jewry had been raised to the fever pitch, when indeed, thousands had parted with all earthly goods because they expected, at any minute, to be miraculously transported to Israel (where Sabbatai

Zevi had already inaugurated the "messianic era"), the pretender to the title of Messiah refused the cup of martyrdom tendered him by the Turkish authorities and was converted to Islam. The sickening impact of this apostasy naturally disillusioned the masses who had acknowledged his claim. But in Eastern Europe, and especially in Poland, the situation that had proved so receptive to his claims persisted, and so, incredibly, did his movement. Those who remained loyal to his name told the people that it was part of a predetermined scheme of salvation that evil had to reach its apogee before God would bless His people with the great good of the final messianic fulfillment. Sabbatai Zevi had, by committing apostasy, done his share; his followers were to do theirs by acting in defiance of all the traditional practices of Judaism, the moral as well as the ceremonial.

The misery of Jewish life in Poland was pretty much unrelieved on into the first half of the eighteenth century, and so the Sabbataian heresy flourished. It remained, for the most part, an underground movement, because the recognized Jewish leadership bitterly resisted its repudiation of Jewish observance. Despite the peculiar potency of the emotional outlet that the Sabbataian cults provided — they offered, among other things, religious sanctions for sexual licentiousness — the great majority of the Jews in Poland were horrified by their excesses, and lived only by the apocalyptic hope for a redemption that would, this time, prove to be genuine.[7]

There were many religious tendencies and movements within the Judaism of the Diaspora. Among these, the one most subject to the influence of apocalyptic messianism was the Jewish mystical tradition, which flourished at various times in many of the countries in which the Jews found themselves. Called the Kabbalah (from the Hebrew "to receive," that is, the received tradition of secret learning), it served as a reservoir of apocalyptic teachings that would, in times of crisis, spread from the few rare spirits who usually studied its secret lore, to the great mass of Jews. The Kabbalah is rooted in teachings that, apparently, antedate the Christian era. During the course of its long history it has manifested the intense spirituality and the speculative fertility of the mystical temperament. However, it had another side, a practical one, that attempted to achieve concrete results within history, and one of the most common of these historical objectives was the effort to hasten the coming of the Messiah. The Sabbataian movement illustrates the weird superstitions and the magical practices that were encouraged by this practical aspect of the Kabbalah.

The Rabbis feared the heretical tendencies of the Kabbalah and they prohibited the teaching of its doctrines in the presence of more than one student. Despite this prohibition, and in spite of the excesses of its practical side, the tradition had, by the time of the Baal Shem Tov, produced a number of profound books which exerted a strong influence on Jewish spirituality.

By domesticating a considerable body of the speculative teachings of the theoretical masters of the Kabbalah, the Baal Shem was able to form a popular religious movement that successfully answered the challenge of the practical aberrations embodied in the messianism of the Sabbataian sects. He infused the speculative systems of the Kabbalah with ethical content and turned the emotional currents of the period into creative Jewish channels. As Buber interprets it, "The Hasidic movement did not weaken hope in a Messiah, but it kindled both its simple and intellectual followers to joy in the world as it is, in life as it is, in every hour of life in this world, as that hour is." [8]

The main techniques embodied in Kabbalistic teachings are familiar to students of mysticism in its many religious guises. They searched the Sacred Scriptures for hidden meanings and, at their best, plumbed depths of religious profundity hitherto undiscerned, although their interpretations frequently contradicted the literal meaning of the texts. The Hebrew and Aramaic in which they wrote encouraged one of the favorite devices of mysticism, the interchange of words according to their numerical value, for Hebrew and Aramaic had no separate numerical system, but used the sequence of the alphabet to form numbers. Thus the letter "a" is one, the letter "b" serves as two, "c" as three, and so on. Once the numerical value of a word had been ascertained, the mystics claimed that it could be interchanged with any word of the same value. For example, the sacred unpronounceable name of God, symbolized by the letters YHVH, had the numerical value of twenty-six and could be substituted for the word "heavy" or any other word that, in its Hebrew spelling, had the same numerical value.

When techniques of this kind were employed by minds of philosophical subtlety, they produced fantastic speculations that purported, in the name of the Bible, to describe the origin of the universe, of man, and of man's estrangement from the divine. Furthermore, by the use of these techniques they attempted to discern the means, hidden from the multitude, whereby the initiate might overcome that estrangement.

The Kabbalists, in common with many other mystics from various religious traditions, generally held the theory that the absolute is a spiritual fullness from which the world as we know it is derived by a process of emanation. That is, successive spheres of being shimmer off the absolute in layers that steadily diminish in spiritual character, ultimately resulting in the world of spirit and matter in which we live. But if the absolute, or as the Kabbalists called it, the En Sof (literally, "Without End" hence the Infinite) is, as the mystics often claim, the totality of being, it is difficult to see how it would be possible for it to emanate, since there is no space outside it.

To deal with this difficulty one of the greatest of the Kabbalists hit upon the daring notion of the Tsim-Tsum. Here the initial act of the En Sof is not regarded as an outgoing act of emanation, but as a sort of contraction, an act of self-limitation. The En Sof draws back into itself, thus leaving space in which the world can emerge as an independent existent.

The process of divine self-contraction may be compared to inhalation. It was to be followed by an act which was rather like exhalation, a beaming of the divine light into the newly created space so that it might be suffused with the divine spirit. To this end, the space had been ordered into a series of bowls or vessels which were to receive the light. But at this point, even before the creation of the world, a disruption of the divine plan occurred. The vessels were unable to contain the divine light and they shattered so that sparks of the light were trapped in the material fragments of the broken vessels. There is a wide range of speculation within the Kabbalistic tradition as to the precise way in which these events finally resulted in the world we know, wherein that disruption of the divine plan is manifest as evil. But they agree that the final result left sparks of the divine light imprisoned in material shells throughout the range of existence. The sparks yearn to return to the divine source from which they have been exiled.[9]

This is the point at which the Baal Shem's creative adaptation of Kabbalism occurs. For this "doctrine of the sparks" binds heaven and earth by teaching that it is up to man to rectify the disruption in the creation. He must, through his actions, liberate or raise the sparks. To this end, the theoreticians of the Kabbalah prescribed an exacting regimen of mystical devotions that only the few could practice. The main effort of the Baal Shem was to bring the people the basic message he distilled from this teaching, namely, that every facet of existence is infused with a spark of the divine; or, to put it another way, that it is permeated by a potential holiness, and that it is up to man, every man, not just the scholar or the mystic, to actualize that potential through his actions.

Of the Hasidic presentation of the doctrine of the sparks, Buber writes:

> There is no reason to fast, as he who eats with devotion redeems the fallen sparks enclosed in the food. . . . There is no reason to do without love of husband or wife, for where a man and woman are together in holy unity, there the Shekhinah [the Divine Presence] rests over them . . . the essential point to Hasidism [is] that man exerts influence on the eternal, and that this is not done by any special works, but by the intention with which he does all his works. It is the teaching of the hallowing of the everyday.[10]

Thus the daily life of the Jew was endowed with redemptive significance, for this act of raising the sparks was understood as a messianic activity that would help to bring about the final consummation — the coming of the Messianic Era. This was the answer that the Baal Shem provided to the Sabbataian cults, which sought to hasten the advent of the Messiah. In this context we can appreciate a Hasidic interpretation of Jacob's dream at Bethel:

> It is written: "And he dreamed, and behold a ladder set up on the earth." That "he" is every man. Every man must know: I am clay, I am one of countless shards of clay, but "the top of it reached to heaven" — my soul reaches to heaven; "and behold the angels of God ascending and descending upon it" — even the ascent and descent of the angels depend upon my deeds.[11]

The most profound Hasidic application of the doctrine of the sparks is to be found in their understanding of love. One Zaddik invoked it to teach his followers that even the wicked must be loved, because, "The soul of every man is a divine particle from above. Even so you have to show pity to God when one holy spark of His has been trapped in a shell." [12] And Buber comments: "Herewith the decisive step has been taken. For as the primeval source of the Deity is linked up with all its soul-sparks which are dispersed throughout the world, so whatever we do to our fellow-men is bound up with what we do to God." So too, Jesus had linked man with God through the medium of love, by quoting the two Mosaic commandments upon which, he said, depended the law and all the prophets: the first, from the book of Deuteronomy, "And thou shalt love the Lord thy God with all thy heart, with all thy soul and with all thy might" (6:5); the second, from the book of Leviticus, ". . . thou shalt love thy neighbor as thyself. . . ." (19:18). In Hasidism, the connection is amplified, and the second is, for purposes of instruction, put before the first.

A Zaddik asked a disciple the following question: "When a Jew arises from bed in the morning and has to choose instantly between two ways, love of God and love of one's neighbor, which should go before the other?" The disciple did not know and so the Zaddik himself answered: "In the Prayer Book it is said, before you say your prayers, you have to recite the verse: 'Love thy neighbor as thyself.' The real love of God should begin with the love of men. And if someone should tell you that he has love of God but has no love of men, then know that he is lying." [13] In this we find a striking echo of the words of the first Epistle of John: "If any man says, I love God, and hates his brother he is a liar; for he who does not love his brother whom he has seen, cannot love God whom he has not seen" (4:20).

Hasidism carries this emphasis on the importance of the second commandment still further, by demonstrating that the two commandments, that we love God and the neighbor, are both contained in the second, which does not end with the phrase "as thyself," but with the words: "I am the Lord." A telling application of this insight is found in the reply which a Zaddik directed to a merchant who complained that a competitor had opened a shop right next to his own.

> "You seem to think," said the Zaddik, "that it is your shop that supports you and you are setting your heart upon it instead of on God who is your support. But perhaps you do not know where God lives? It is written: 'Love thy neighbor as thyself: I am the Lord.' This means: 'you shall want for your neighbor what he needs just as you do for yourself — and therein you will find the Lord.' " [14]

Buber's interpretation of the biblical commandment to love the neighbor — which proceeds along these same lines — provides an excellent illustration of the way in which Hasidic and biblical teachings have interacted with his own dialogic philosophy. Buber examines the key phrase, generally translated "to your neighbor as yourself," and observes: "The word so translated refers neither to the degree nor the kind of love, as if a man should love others as much as himself or in such a way as himself . . . it means, equal to thyself, and this means: conduct thyself in such a way as if it concerned thyself. An attitude is meant and not a feeling." [15] Love involves the I-Thou attitude, that turning to the other which is the heart of dialogue. In this relation, the other, bodied over against the self, is recognized as a unique person, by a self that knows itself to be unique.

Much of Hasidism can be understood as a reaction to, and an adaptation of, the teachings of the Kabbalah. But, whatever its merits and shortcomings, the Kabbalah was never the main element of Judaism. It was the Rabbinic tradition that, for over two thousand years, maintained the unity and integrity of Judaism, first in Palestine and then in the many countries of the Diaspora.

The heart of this tradition is Torah, an untranslatable term, generally rendered as Law, but more properly understood as divinely ordained commandment and teaching, as instruction directing a people to holiness.[16] The primary and most authoritative literary source of the Torah, the Pentateuch, was regarded as the source of all truth; but it required explication and interpretation. For example, the fourth of the Ten Commandments, which enjoins the people to keep the Sabbath rest by refraining from all work on the seventh day of each week, does not specify the activities that are to be regarded as work. Problems of this order were resolved by an Oral Tradition of interpretation, which, apparently, emerged at an early period in the history of Israel; it is called the Oral Torah.

At the close of the biblical epoch a professional class of interpreters — known by many technical terms, although for our purpose the generic term "Rabbi" will suffice — formalized this tradition. They established schools of Torah study in which generations of disciples memorized learned discussions. In time, many of these were recorded — a crucial step in extending a unified Rabbinic authority outside of Palestine. Indeed, the most influential collection of Rabbinic materials — recording discussions that were held over a period ranging from 200 B.C. to A.D. 500 — is the *Babylonian* Talmud (from a word meaning study), which has a lesser known Palestinian counterpart. These, and the other compilations of materials of that era, constitute the classical texts of Rabbinic teaching. They have been authoritative for Judaism through the centuries. They remain the authoritative texts through whose eyes the ultimate root of divine revelation, the Jewish Bible, is read by Orthodox Jews today. Although adherents of the other branches of organized Judaism may reject their authority, they nevertheless revere them.

The many volumes of the Rabbinic literature contain two fundamental types of material. The Halachah, a term derived from the word for "path," prescribes the path the Jew is to follow in order to fulfill the will of God. It consists of legal deliberations in which the Rabbis, with great acumen, define the precise details of observance of the Mosaic injunctions. This Halachic activity was authoritative. The Jew was required to conduct himself in accordance with the findings of the Rabbis, because their learning qualified them to elaborate the Torah which was given at Sinai. There was no question of their being endowed with supernatural powers and no miracles validated their teachings.

The other class of Rabbinic materials is called Haggadah,* "narration," and the name suggests its popular approach. The Rabbis used all the wisdom of their times in an effort to search the Jewish Bible for every nuance of meaning. The result was a body of moral and religious teachings whose contents were readily accessible to the people. But while the Haggadic teachings were honored, used a great deal in preaching, and very much loved, in contrast to the teachings of the Halachah, they were not authoritative. Although a unified moral and theological atmosphere emerges from Haggadic teachings, the many specific contradictions between the outlook of one Rabbi and another were not resolved by subsequent interpretation. The kind of consistency that characterized Halachic teachings was not regarded as necessary, or even as desirable, for those of the Haggadah, because the latter did not define matters of practice.

Torah-interpretation did not cease with the close of the Talmudic era. The problems involved in understanding the Talmudic texts, and the need to relate the Halachah to the changing circumstances of Jewish life evoked commentaries on the Talmudic texts from the scholars of every generation. In turn, commentaries were written on the more significant commentaries of previous generations, and the process continues to the present day. Those who have dismissed this activity as a sterile form of casuistry in which the snake of Rabbinic disquisition feeds upon its own tail,

* The Passover Haggadah is a special case; it contains many things besides Haggadic literature.

miss a crucial point. The Rabbis have regarded the Torah as the greatest gift that God has given man; its study, and the refinements of practice that proceed from that study, are the deepest form of devotion available to traditional Jewish piety.

A clue to the vitality of post-biblical Judaism is to be found in the fact that all the commentaries on the Jewish Bible and the Rabbinic literature that have been written through the centuries, including those that are being written today, are revered as part of the Oral Torah — of the chain of living tradition.

Although the devoted scholarship of the Rabbis was one of Judaism's great glories, it was always possible for it to lead to intellectual and religious snobbery on the part of the learned. This tendency was normally held in check by the relatively high level of learning, compared to that of the laity of most religions, attained by Jewish congregations. This left the Rabbis little excuse for that condescension toward the simple faith of the masses that haunts the professionals of most religions. However, in the Eastern Europe of the eighteenth century, the upheavals of the persecutions and of the Sabbataian movements which followed them all but eliminated this counterweight to the intellectualizing tendencies of the Rabbis. By the time of the Baal Shem Tov they had converted the discipline of Torah study into a complex logical activity that had much in common with chess; it was utterly divorced from everyday life, and only the most brilliant could play well enough to make it worthwhile. Furthermore, the prestige of the scholars became so great that they constituted a social and religious, as well as an intellectual, aristocracy.

The Baal Shem challenged this abuse of the Rabbinic

tradition by teaching that the inequalities which existed in the outer realm of human affairs could not penetrate to the core of man's relation to God. The simple man of genuine piety stood higher than those whose learning led them to undue pride.[17] Hasidism produced many stories celebrating the devotion of ordinary people who did not spend their time in study. Of these, the most significant, because it relates to an experience which was typical of so many of the Jews of his time, is the Baal Shem's word on the response of a business man to the obligation, incumbent upon every Jew each day, to recite the afternoon prayers of the Jewish liturgy.

> "Imagine a man whose business hounds him through many streets and across the market-place the livelong day. He almost forgets that there is a Maker of the world. Only when the time for the Afternoon Prayer comes, does he remember: 'I must pray.' And then, from the bottom of his heart, he heaves a sigh of regret that he has spent his day on vain and idle matters, and he runs into a by-street and stands there, and prays: God holds him dear, very dear, and his prayer pierces the firmament." [18]

All religions espouse beliefs and prescribe actions that are supposed to bring the faithful into proper relation to the absolute. And all inevitably obscure this ultimate purpose by emphasizing their creeds and rituals to such a degree that they become an end in themselves. In traditional Judaism this "absolutizing of the relative" takes the form of legalism, that is, of forgetting that the Torah is instruction whose purpose is to bring the total life of the Jew into proper relation to God; instead, it makes the proper performance of the acts prescribed by the Halachah the focus of piety. The question of the motivation for the performance of these acts is relegated to the background or treated in the crassest terms; neglect of them leads to damnation; proper performance, regardless of the inner attitude, guarantees salvation.

Unfortunately, through the centuries, Christian polemicists have conveyed the impression that the essential teaching of Judaism is legalistic. To appreciate the thoroughly distorted picture of Jewish teaching that has been prevalent in Western culture, one must also consider the wide influence of the Gospel portrait of the Pharisees, the founders of the Talmudic tradition, as sanctimonious hypocrites caring nothing for the spirit but only for the letter of the Torah (misconstrued as Law). Today this distortion is being corrected. Both Christian and Jewish scholars have written numerous works portraying the Rabbis of the Talmud as men who well knew the distinction between the letter and the spirit, and as men whose deepest drive was to see that Judaism embodied the latter.

It is a good thing that the distortions of Jewish teaching are being rectified. But enthusiasm for this salutory development ought not to blind us to the fact that in every age there have been Jews who behaved as though the external act was so important in itself that the motivation hardly mattered. "Indeed," says Buber, "the constant danger of the form of faith which tends to the realization of a revealed divine will, is that the keeping of it can persist apart from the intended surrender to the divine will. . . . The beginnings of this process of making the gesture independent go back to the early times of the Sinai-religion. The struggle against it runs through the whole history of Israelite-Jewish faith." [19] The Prophets protested against sacrifices, which loomed so large in the minds of the people that they took the place of God, and the Hasidim were part of this same tradition of protest. They warned the people against making the performance of Halachic prescriptions into an absolute, into a false god.

> The disciples of the Rabbi of Kotzk were once discussing why it is written: "Take heed unto yourselves, lest ye forget the covenant of the Lord your God, which he made with you, and make you a graven image, even in the likeness of any thing which the Lord thy God hath *bidden* thee," and not — as the meaning really demands — "which the Lord thy God hath *forbidden* thee." The Zaddik who had been listening, joined in the discussion. "The Torah warns us," said he, "not to make a graven image of any thing the Lord our God has *bidden* us." [20]

In his earliest interpretations of Judaism, Buber made the common mistake of treating legalism as the Rabbinic ideal rather than as an abuse of its teaching. Later, without ceasing to criticize the legalism that is actually to be found in Judaism, he came to see that there is a profound appreciation of the significance of motivation in the Talmudic literature itself. The Rabbis teach that acts of Torah are to be performed *Lishmah*, that is, "for the sake of the Name," the holy name of God, and not for hope of reward or fear of punishment. "The only thing which matters," Buber observes, "is that everything should be done truly for God's sake, from love to Him and in love to Him." [21]

At their best, the Hasidim lived *Lishmah*. When one of the Zaddikim was a young boy, his father, who thought that he had been gambling when he had actually been studying the Torah intensely, beat him till he bled.

> "And did you not tell your father that you were studying all that time?" they asked [him] when he told the story many years after.
>
> "I might have told him, of course," he answered. "And my father would have believed me, for he knew that I never lied, but is it right to use the greatness of the Torah to save one's own skin?" [22]

As one of the most elaborate aspects of Jewish observance, the dietary laws readily evoke legalistic attitudes from the faithful. Countless volumes have been written concerning *Kashruth,* the ceremonial or ritual purity of food and of the utensils relating to its preparation and consumption. One of the most impressive Hasidic protests against legalism, which is reminiscent of the teaching in Matthew (15:10–20), deals with the contrast between the ceremonial purity of meat and the inner purity of the believer. It begins when a Zaddik tells his chief disciple, Rabbi Bunam, to go on a journey with a number of Hasidim. The Zaddik gave no reason for the excursion and mentioned no destination. Bunam, puzzled but obedient, departed with the group. After a while they came to an inn whose proprietor was delighted to receive the patronage of the "pious ones."

> Rabbi Bunam sat down in the main room, while the other went in and out and asked all sorts of questions concerning the meat which was to be served them: whether the animal was unblemished, what the butcher was like, and just how carefully the meat had been salted.
>
> At that a man dressed in rags spoke up. He had been sitting behind the stove and still had his staff in his hand. "O you Hasidim," he said, "you make a big to-do about what you put into your mouths being clean, but you don't worry half as

> much about the purity of what comes out of your mouths!"
>
> Rabbi Bunam was about to reply, but the wayfarer had already disappeared — for this is Elijah's habit [since he did not die but ascended to heaven in a fiery chariot, returning to earth frequently to play a role in Jewish folklore]. Then the Rabbi understood why his teacher had sent him on this journey.[23]

Many of the Hasidic stories rebuke those who display excessive concern for the external details of the actions enjoined by the Halachah. In one of them a young man tells a Zaddik of his great remorse at having failed to read some of the prescribed portions of the Torah during a religious service.

> Later the Rabbi said to his friends: "There's your superpious man! All he cares about is doing exactly what is prescribed. But he whose soul is directed toward doing the will of God within the commandment, and clings wholly to God's will, may very possibly fail to do something of what is prescribed, but it does not trouble him. For it is written: 'In thy love for her wilt thou err constantly.' "[24]

Variations in the performance of acts of Torah were not only permitted by the early Hasidic leaders; their emphasis on motivation actually encouraged variations. When the Hasidim were criticized because they did not pray at set times, a Zaddik answered that soldiers in training must do everything on schedule, but that in battle they forget what is prescribed and fight as the hour demands. " 'The Hasidim,' he added, "are fighters."[25] When two Hasidim whose master had died came to join the community of another Zaddik, they were shocked at his variations from the practices of their former leader. Noticing this, the Zaddik said, "A God whom one could serve only in one set way — what kind of a God would that be!" [26] Buber concludes that in early Hasidism we find, "A teaching which sets the winged 'How' of an act high above the codified 'What' . . ." [27]

But Hasidism was not concerned merely with suffusing the prescribed acts of Torah with proper intention — it went further. According to both its teaching and practice the decisive factor in expressing devotion to God was not the performance of acts which had been Halachically defined. It was the consecration of all acts of everyday life to God — that is, the hallowing of this life and this world. Out of the many examples of hallowing acts of service that are to be found in the two volumes of Buber's *Tales of the Hasidim*, the following one best illustrates the tenderness the Zaddikim could bring to them, and also illustrates the way in which the acts of service could take precedence over the official religious obligations.

> On the eve of the Day of Atonement, when the time had come to say Kol Nidre [the most solemn moment of prayer in the Jewish year] all the Hasidim were gathered together in the House of Prayer waiting for the Rabbi. But time passed and he did not come. Then one of the women of the congregation said to herself: "I guess it will be quite a while before they begin, and I was in such a hurry and my child is alone in the house. I'll just run home and look after it to make sure it hasn't awakened. I can be back in a few minutes."
>
> She ran home and listened at the door. Everything was quiet. Softly she turned the knob and put her head into the room — and there stood the Rabbi holding her child in his arms. He had heard the

> child crying on his way to the House of Prayer, and played with it and sung to it until it fell asleep.[28]

The Zaddikim were great men of the spirit, but when their function was institutionalized it led to the formation of aristocratic dynasties that were regarded with awe by the simple groups of Jews who acknowledged their leadership. Initially, Buber claims, the Zaddikim did not stand in a lordly relation to their followers; they acted as their guides to the life of hallowing.[29] They were ready to help their followers cope with any problem, but not in a way that relieved these ordinary men of their responsibilities. The Zaddikim sought to lead them to a point at which they themselves would respond genuinely to each other and to God. They sought to awaken them to the hallowing potential of their everyday routines. When a disciple begged God to give him a good living in order that he might not be hindered in the study of Torah, his Zaddik told him: ". . . what God really wants of you is not study or prayer, but the sighs of your heart, which is breaking because the travail of gaining a livelihood hinders you in the service of God." [30]

These Hasidic tales provide a striking confirmation of Buber's fundamental declaration that, "To man the world is twofold, in accordance with his twofold attitude." [31] Seen from the I-Thou attitude, the story just quoted shows a Zaddik leading a disciple to a vital relation to God by showing him that God is not so much interested in the performance of "sacred offices" as He is in the intention of the individual to fulfill His will amid the routines of daily life. Seen from the detachment of the I-It attitude, the story may serve as an excellent example of the sort of thing that engenders the

Marxist criticism of religion. A religious leader tells a poor man, burdened by the misery of his existence, that God appreciates his poverty! The reader will find that all the stories lend themselves to the same twofold treatment, though, of course, the perspective we adopt in the attitude of detachment need not be a Marxist one.

The point of this flexibility of interpretation is that the life of faith cannot be sustained by a retreat from the intellectual difficulties involved in a religious world-view. On the contrary, faith is distinguished from fanaticism by the fact that it exists in "holy insecurity," in the tension between the affirmations afforded in the posture of engagement, and the doubts engendered in the moments of detachment.[32]

By teaching the man of simple faith the hallowing potential of his actions the Zaddikim assured each and every one of them that, "The world in which you live, just as it is and not otherwise, affords you that association with God, which will redeem you and whatever divine aspect of the world you have been entrusted with. And your own character, the very qualities which make you what you are, constitutes your special approach to God, your special potential use for Him." [33]

Nor was this teaching a consolation prize for the great mass of simple followers of the Zaddikim; the Zaddikim, or at least some of them, applied it to themselves. One of them put it this way, "David could compose the Psalms, and what can I do? I can recite the Psalms." [34] Before his death, the saintly Rabbi Zusya made this same point, "In the coming world, they will not ask me: 'Why were you not Moses?' They will ask me: 'Why were you not Zusya?' " [35]

Yet it is not enough for the hallowing acts that constitute each man's special use for God to be done out of love for

Him; they must also be performed with fervor. Fervent piety was the quality that first attracted Buber to the Hasidic teachings when he encountered it in the utterance of the Baal Shem about rising eagerly from sleep.[36] The Hasidim expressed their fervor in many ways, the most colorful being in song and dance. In one instance a story is told of an aged lame Hasid who attempted to describe the way in which the Baal Shem had hopped and danced in prayer. He was swept away with enthusiasm and began to leap about himself, and he was cured.[37] In another story the wife of a Zaddik reproves her husband for allowing a lame pupil (who later became a Zaddik) to pound on the floor with both feet while praying. "Tell him to use only his good foot," she said. "I could do that right enough," answered the Zaddik, "if, in praying he knew every time whether he was using his good or his bad foot." [38]

At first blush, the Hasidic emphasis on the quality of fervor might seem to contradict its emphasis on working steadily toward the hallowing of all acts by each and every man in his everyday life. In practice, however, it is the main support of this attitude, because it teaches men to see, feel, and live the holy in the midst of lives encumbered with the burden of routine.

> God says to man, as he said to Moses: "Put off thy shoes from thy feet" — put off the habitual which encloses your foot, and you will know that the place on which you are now standing is holy ground. For there is no rung of human life on which we cannot find the holiness of God everywhere and at all times.[39]

Far from constituting an exception to the Hasidic emphasis on hallowing the everyday life, the emphasis upon fervor greatly intensifies it. For it distinguishes Hasidism from otherworldly religions, which present a fundamentally dualistic view of reality. These religions propagandize the view that the "Lord of this life" is a God who not only permits suffering but who inflicts it on the faithful. Man's chief virtue lies in passive acceptance of life as a "vale of tears." In the after-life, the other side of reality which they set in contrast to this one, all this is reversed and the faithful enjoy everlasting bliss from the hands of an eternally benevolent deity. But this absolute disjunction at the heart of reality is not convincing. A God who is known in this life as a God of judgment alone, could hardly be expected to be pure love in the next one. Similarly, a man who has spent his life in crabbed rejection of all the joys it affords will hardly emerge as a world-affirming creature in some future existence. Hasidism, against all the negative emphasis of otherworldly religions, has insisted that true piety involves fervent rejoicing in the here and now, for if not now, then never.

> If a man has fulfilled all the commandments, he is admitted to the Garden of Eden [i.e. Heaven], even though he has not burned with fervor and has not experienced delight. But since he has felt no delight on earth, he feels none there either. Finally, he even grumbles: "And they make all that to-do about paradise!" And hardly have the words left his lips, when he is thrown out! [40]

Just as Hasidism affirmed the community as a whole, without excluding the man of simple faith, so it affirmed man as a whole without excluding his bodily nature in the name of his "higher," that is, his intellectual, faculties. The quality of fervor united all vital energies — physical, emotional, and intellectual—in service to God. Every part of man and everything that he does is to be dedicated to the holy work of restoring the sparks to their divine source. And so, a Hasid, on being asked, "What was most important to your teacher?" was able to answer, "Whatever he happened to be doing at the moment." [41]

This emphasis on wholeness, on the unity of teaching and virtue, enabled Hasidism, at its best, to overcome the gap between theory and practice that has marred the history of so many religious movements. One of the Zaddikim spoke disparagingly of Rabbis who were proud of the subtlety with which they expounded the Torah: "What does it amount to—their expounding the Torah! A man should see to it that all his actions are a Torah and that he himself becomes so entirely a Torah that one can learn from his habits and his motions and his motionless clinging to God." [42] A disciple of the Maggid ("preacher") of Mezritch, the most learned master of Torah among the Baal Shem Tov's immediate circle of followers, said: "I did not go to the Maggid in order to hear Torah from him, but to see how he unlaces his felt shoes and laces them up again." [43]

Buber acknowledges a difficulty in his presentation of Hasidism as a movement that, by affirming every aspect of life, seeks to overcome the distinction between the sacred and the profane. To the outsider, Judaism, with its elaborate mass of observances, seems to separate the two more sharply than almost any other religion. What other meaning could be attached to the dietary laws, which are defined with such incredible detail in order to make certain that the ceremonially pure is separated from the contaminated? What other meaning could be attached to the mass of priestly doctrines of purity and impurity, which the Rabbis studied even after the destruction of the Second Temple rendered them obsolete? And it would seem that the clinching argument is provided by the prayer ending the Sabbath; in it the Jew addresses God as, "the One who separates the sacred from the profane." [44]

Buber answers that Hasidism more than any other aspect of Judaism, teaches the provisional character of the distinction between the sacred and the profane. "Hasidic piety no longer recognizes anything as simply and irreparably profane: 'the profane' is for Hasidism only a designation for the not yet sanctified, for that which is to be sanctified. Everything physical, all drives and urges and desires, everything creaturely, is material for sanctification." [45]

One of the Zaddikim interpreted the verse from the Psalms, "The heavens are the heavens of the Lord, but the earth hath He given to the children of men" (Ps 115:16), to mean that, whereas the heavens are already heavenly, man has been given the task of making the earth into something heavenly.[46] And this insight is incorporated into Buber's most eloquent summary of Hasidic teachings:

> The Hasidic teaching is the consummation of Judaism. And this is its message to all: *You yourself must begin.* Existence will remain meaningless for you if you yourself do not penetrate into it with active love and if you do not in this way discover its meaning for yourself. Everything is waiting to be hallowed by you; it is waiting to be disclosed in its meaning and to be realized in it by you. For the sake of this your beginning, God created the world. He has drawn it out of Himself so that you may bring it closer to Him. Meet the world with the fullness of your being and you shall meet Him. That He Himself accepts from your hands what you have to give to the world, is His mercy. If you wish to believe, love! [47]

6. The Mission of Judaism

ALTHOUGH religions urge men to concentrate on the permanently significant aspects of existence and to lay less emphasis on ephemeral goods, men persist in focusing their attention on the treasures of this earth, which moth and rust consume. In reaction to this obdurate concentration on the transitory, religions often adopt the twofold strategy of withdrawal and asceticism. They call on their followers to withdraw from what the New Testament calls "the world," that is, from the sphere of cultural, political, and even economic concerns, which relate to the larger units of human association. To insure the members of the withdrawn community against further traffic with the world and its pleasures, they also counsel the faithful to follow ascetic practices, that is, to subdue their passions and to live by the spirit alone.

In Western civilization these two strategies have always resulted in the emergence of a vast gulf between the domain of God and that of Caesar. This is reflected in the very word "religion," as it is used in the modern world; it has come to mean an association of those who agree on certain "spiritual" beliefs and practices. Martin Buber has always opposed this kind of religion; he holds that ". . . the realer religion is, so much the more it means its own overcoming. It wills to cease to be the special domain 'Religion' and wills to become life."[1]

This attitude toward religion illustrates the thoroughly Jewish character of Buber's thought. He insists, quite rightly, that Judaism is not a religion in this modern sense of the term. It does not confine itself to "spiritual" matters, but seeks to bring the totality of life under God. Judaism does not urge its followers to withdraw from "the world," it urges them to affirm the world by hallowing it. It does not espouse an ascetic abjuration of the pleasures of the flesh but teaches that these too must be sanctified.[2] The patriarchal ideal expressed so vividly in the book of Genesis and in the opening lines of the book of Job is that of a long life, rich in devotion to God, and blessed with numerous children and many possessions. It remains an authentically Jewish ideal to this day.

Early in his career Buber thought of this world-affirming aspect of Judaism as the work of its creative leaders — the prophets, mystics, and heretics who, in his view, radically opposed the rigid formalism of the official leaders of the cult — the priests, and the Rabbis.[3] As he acquired a greater familiarity with Jewish teachings Buber modified this sharp dichotomy and came to regard the two most vital Jewish forces, the prophetic faith and the teachings of Hasidism, as concentrated forms of an outlook that is to be found throughout Judaism.[4] He retreated so far from the radicalism of his early years that he even came to see the Pharisees, those initiators of the Rabbinic tradition, as one of the most creative forces in the history of Jewish faith. They brought the written words of the Torah into meaningful relation to the everyday life of their time by adopting them to changing circumstances. Although Buber has never abandoned his conviction that the Rabbis of later ages codified the work of the Pharisees and converted it into a rigid Orthodoxy, he insists that the Pharisees themselves, far from devitalizing Judaism, preserved the basic world-affirming posture of the prophetic faith. And they did this at a time when many Jews succumbed to the world-negating tendencies that were prevalent among the various dualistic religions of that period.

The Rabbis of the Talmudic era taught that man has two basic urges or inclinations, the *yetzer hatov*, the inclination to good, and the *yetzer harah*, the inclination to the evil. Had the Rabbis adopted the world-denying outlook so common to the religions of their age they would have taught the Jews to purge themselves of the evil inclination; instead, they held that the evil inclination was a necessary part of man. It is the power behind his impulse to marry, beget children, build homes, and to engage in economic activities. Some Rabbis went as far as teaching that the evil inclination itself could be regarded as good, since in the first chapter of Genesis it is written: "And God saw every thing that He had made, and, behold, it was very good" (1:31).[5]

The evil urge, Buber comments, is not then evil in itself. It is only evil insofar as it prevents a man from directing his entire being toward God, that is, from being motivated by the love of God in all his actions. He writes that according to this teaching, "Man's task . . . is not to extirpate the evil urge, but to reunite it with the good."[6] And, he later adds that, "To unite the two urges implies: to equip the absolute potency of passion with the one direction that renders it capable of great love and of great service. Thus and not otherwise can one become whole."[7] Buber's understanding of the nature of evil and of man's capacity for overcoming it, owes much to this Rabbinic teaching, and to the Hasidic version of it, "From the very same passionate powers which, undirected, gave rise to evil, when they are turned toward God, the good arises." [8]

Human nature is, by virtue of man's freedom, paradoxical. Man grows, but not in the simple way that an animal grows; he must choose and strive to become that which he truly is. He must relate himself to the world in a way that enables him to actualize his unique potential. "In a period of evolution, which generally coincides with puberty without being tied to it, the human person inevitably becomes aware of the category of possibility, which of all living creatures is represented just in man, manifestly the only one for whom the real is continually fringed by the possible." [9]

The possibilities that surround the individual induce a dizziness like that of the talented student who must finally choose one career after distinguishing himself in many areas. Each decision closes the door to possibilities, and each decision imposes new responsibilities. Buber says, "It is a cruelly hazardous enterprise this becoming whole, becoming a form, . . . [this] crystallization of the soul." [10] Many people never really embark on it. They seem to be involved in a process of decision but, since they lack a sense of direction from which to make their decisions, what is really involved is a clutching at chance factors that loom large at one moment or another. This series of pseudo-decisions results in a life that follows the line of least resistance. Initially evil is not as much an act as it is this negative state of drifting, of failing to choose the good; the specific acts of evil—grasping, devouring, compelling, exploiting, humiliating, and the rest — follow from it.[11]

Once started, evil builds up momentum. This is illustrated by two of the most provocative texts in the Jewish Bible which describe God as acting on the human heart: He 'hardens' the heart of the Pharoah so that he will not permit Israel to go into the wilderness to worship Him, and He 'fattens' the hearts of the Israelites so that they will not respond to the message He sends through His servant Isaiah. As Buber understands them, these texts do not refer to a supernatural action that overrides the human will, but rather, they show, ". . . that sin is not an undertaking which man can break off when the situation becomes critical, but a process started by him the control of which is withdrawn from him at a fixed moment." [12] Here Buber is saying that, if a man involved in evil does not continually try to turn to the good, he finally reaches a point where he loses all capacity for making the effort to turn, and he consciously chooses radical evil. This is, ". . . man's endeavor to render the contradictory state, which has arisen in consequence of his lack of direction and his psuedo-decisions, bearable and even satisfying, by affirming this state, in the context of the total constitution of his personality, absolutely." [13]

This is all very abstract, and it may be helpful to consider George Eliot's *Romola*, a novel whose central character, a young scholar named Tito Melema, is delineated in terms that constitute one of the most incisive studies of evil to be found in literature. He arrives in the Florence of the late fifteenth century with a handsome face, an attractive personality, and a bag of jewels.

The jewels are the "forbidden fruit" of the story, since they do not belong to Tito, but are the property of Baldassare, his foster father. The two had been separated at sea when pirates raided their ship. Tito had escaped because of his marvellous ability as a swimmer, but it was quite likely that Baldassare had been captured and sold into slavery. It was Tito's intention, when he arrived in Florence, to sell the jewels and to use the money to search for his foster father. Tito was fully conscious of the debt of gratitude he owed Baldassare, who had found him living in miserable conditions when Tito was seven years old, and had adopted him and raised him with great devotion.

But Tito, instead of setting out to seek Baldassare at once, procrastinates from day to day. In the meantime his personality and talent enable him to gain the patronage of leading citizens and to win the love of a beautiful woman. As he moves from one conquest to another, Tito never decides against setting out to rescue Baldassare, he postpones the decision with rationalizations, by thinking that Baldassare may have drowned or that, by staying in Florence, he will be more likely to get reliable information about him.

When Tito sells the jewels for a very good price, the moment of decision is thrust upon him, for the merchant who buys them offers to deposit the money to Tito's great advantage, and Tito accepts. Buber's analysis is most relevant. Tito had never decided to embark on a course of evil, he had failed to decide for a clearly defined good, and then fell into evil when he clutched at this chance that presented itself.

The process of evil starts by his failure to use the money as a means of starting a search for his foster father. Tito then falls into a pattern of dishonor whose culmination is reached when Baldassare, who had indeed been captured, and, after some months, entered Florence as a slave, escapes his captors and suddenly stumbles upon his foster son standing in the company of some influential friends. Once again Tito impulsively seizes the chance possibility of the moment instead of the decision for the good. He turns from Baldassare's beseeching glance and tells his friends that the stranger is a madman, thereby protecting himself against the possibility of Baldassare's denunciations.

This is the last act of evil that Tito commits impulsively. From that moment on, driven by the fear that his treachery will be discovered, his evil is one of calculated choice. In the new stage of radical evil he consciously exploits the attractiveness of his personality to gain the confidence of leading figures in the various parties that were struggling for control of Florence, and he betrays them all.

Buber has used other terms to designate the stages of evil as we find them illustrated in the character of Tito Melema. He has called the first stage of evil the way of the sinners who again and again miss God's way through their failure to direct themselves toward the good. The stage of radical evil is that of the wicked who oppose God's way with the basic attitude of their being. The way to righteousness, Buber observes, is not closed to them from God's side, ". . . but it is closed from the side of the wicked themselves. For in distinction from the sinners they do not wish to be able to turn."[14]

The stage of radical evil, the way of the wicked, did not suggest itself readily to Buber. In the earliest years of his thinking on the subject he was inclined to treat evil in less far-reaching terms. It was the experience of the first World War, and the shocking circumstances connected with the killing of his friend Gustave Landauer, that forced him to the recognition of a deeper dimension of evil than he had hitherto imagined. The subsequent history of the twentieth century has confirmed, all too conclusively, his insight into the radical character of evil.[15]

His attitude toward evil and the general temper of the man himself are strikingly revealed in a speech Buber delivered in Frankfurt-am-Main in 1953 when he received the Peace Prize of the German Book Trade. Accepting this award, and one other from a different German institution, with the memories of the Nazi era still fresh, were the two most controversial acts of his career. Buber performed them knowing that he would be bitterly condemned in Jewish circles, and in many non-Jewish ones as well. But his Frankfurt address to the German people is one of the most moving documents of our time and it provides an effective statement of his reasons for accepting the awards. The address begins with a rejection of the totalitarian thinking that is so typical of our age — and not only in totalitarian countries.

> From my youth on I have taken the real existence of peoples most seriously. But I have never, in the face of any historical moment, past or present, allowed the concrete multiplicity existing at that moment within a people . . . to be obscured by the levelling concept of a totality constituted and acting in just such a way and no other.[16]

This observation led him to a reflection on the variety to be found among the Germans living under Nazi rule. He divided them into three groups. The members of the first are to be numbered with the righteous. This group consists of those who, on learning of what was taking place, killed themselves because they found that they could do nothing to overcome the evil, and of those who tried to overcome it and were killed by the regime. "I see these men very near before me in that especial intimacy which binds us at times to the dead and to them alone. Reverence and love for these Germans now fills my heart." [17]

The second group is composed of those who did not know what was happening and, dreading the truth, took no pains to discover it, as well as of those who, knowing the truth, still did not oppose the evil. These are the sinners, the great majority who drift along with each other. Of them Buber writes, ". . . my heart, which is acquainted with the weakness of men, refuses to condemn my neighbor for not prevailing upon himself to become a martyr." [18]

The third group are the wicked; and here radical evil is manifested with unparalleled, even unimaginable, ferocity. Buber's words to the German people regarding this group were epochal, and the more so for the restraint exercised in his statement of their crime.

> About a decade ago a considerable number of Germans — there must have been many thousands of them — under the indirect command of the German government and the direct command of its representatives, killed millions of my people in a systematically prepared and executed procedure whose organized cruelty cannot be compared with any previous historical event.

Then follows his statement of his response:

> I, who am one of those who remained alive, have only in a formal sense a common humanity with those who took part in this action. They have so radically removed themselves from the human sphere, so transposed themselves into a sphere of monstrous inhumanity inaccessible to my conception, that not even hatred, much less an overcoming of hatred, was able to arise in me. And what am I that I could here presume to "forgive!" [19]

The wicked man wilfully cuts himself off from God and removes himself from humanity, but most men are sinners and for them there is always the possibility of the *teshuvah*, "the turning to God." This has been a central category of Jewish piety from the time of the Prophets, through the teaching of the Talmud, and on into the modern era. Whether addressing himself to the Jewish community in terms of the divine charge to Israel, or to modern man in terms of the possibilities of the renewal of dialogue, Buber has never ceased to call for the turning.[20]

The first step, the true beginning, is the recognition that all is not well. Here the Rabbis are at one with Jesus who justified the fact that he consorted with sinners by saying that the physician comes to heal the sick and not those who are well.[21] Implicit in this statement is the warning that those who think themselves well are even more sick, because they do not realize how gravely they stand in need of the physician. The Baal Shem Tov's statement of this teaching is more detailed than its New Testament counterpart:

> "I let sinners come close to me, if they are not proud. I keep the scholars and the sinless away from me if they are proud. For the sinner who knows he is a sinner, and therefore considers himself base — God is with him, for He 'dwelleth with them in the midst of their uncleannesses.' But concerning him who prides himself on the fact that he is unburdened by sin, God says, as we know from the Gemara [literally, "completion," the final stratum of the Talmud]: 'There is not enough room in the world for myself and him.' "[22]

The New Testament characterizes the Pharisees as sanctimonious hypocrites and claims that they were bitterly censorious of Jesus' attitude toward sinners. In light of this, it is ironical that the Pharisees should themselves have promulgated a teaching that expresses the point of the parable of the Prodigal Son: "In the place where those who have turned stand, the perfectly righteous cannot stand." [23] And when some Hasidim, like the older brother in the parable, protested against the injustice involved in a teaching that sets the man who has sinned much and turned, above the man who has never strayed from the true path, their Zaddak answered:

> "He who sees a new light every day, light he did not see the day before, if he wishes truly to serve, must condemn his imperfect service of yesterday, atone for it, and start afresh. The stainless one who believes he has done perfect service, and persists in it, does not accept the light, and comes after him who ever turns anew." [24]

Buber is concerned to distinguish the turning from the phenomenon of repentance with which it might otherwise be readily identified. Repentance is an inner state that is necessary to the turning, but turning should be understood in the literal sense as a directing of the entire self into dialogical relation with all beings, and so into relation with the eternal Thou. Just as Judaism will not reject any part of the world, since in each and every being there is a spark of the divine waiting for the hallowing act of man, so too, it will not reject any part of man, holding that the hallowing act can only be performed by the whole man. "The primary word I-Thou can only be spoken with the whole being." [25]

The great leaders of Judaism have always cried, "Turn ye." But, while the Jew must accomplish the turning in his own life, he does so as a member of the covenantal community and not as an isolated individual. Buber's own outlook, which is permeated with Jewish teachings, could not and does not fail to display that passionate concern for the establishment of genuine community that is so integral a part of the mission of Judaism.

Buber's devotion to the vision of genuine community has found its fullest and most impassioned expressions in his writings on Zionism. In the earliest ones, written at the turn of the century under the influence of Nietzsche and romanticism, he regarded Judaism as a channel for the creative energies of the individual Jew. The channel was forged by the tie of blood that bound the individual to the spirit of his people as it is manifest in the dead, the living, and even in those yet unborn.[26]

This emphasis on the overwhelming significance of the blood tie and on the peculiar gifts of the people who were bound together by it, was tragically misappropriated in the anti-Jewish polemic of the Nazi philosopher Alfred Rosenberg. By the time the Nazis rallied the German people to their degenerate form of blood and soil romanticism, Buber had abandoned this sort of glorification of the folk-character of peoples. Under the influence of Hasidism and of other Jewish teachings, he had come to see the significance of Israel in terms of the fidelity of the people to the Covenant that God had established with their fathers and to regard Zionism, the drive to establish a Jewish State, as a means for realizing the prophetic vision of a community of justice and peace. Instead of being concerned with what Judaism could contribute to the creative energies of the individual Jew, Buber concentrated on communicating the Hasidic teaching that God waits for man to complete His work of creation by hallowing the world.

Although the teachings that the Hasidic masters adapted from Rabbinic and Kabbalistic sources were an important part of the greatness of this movement, they were only a commentary upon the central reality: the genuine communities Hasidism established throughout the villages of Eastern Europe. Of this central reality Buber writes:

> Let it be noted: it does not form a fraternity, it does not form a separate order, which guards an esoteric teaching, apart from public life; it forms a community, it forms a community of people; these people continue living their life within their family, rank, public activity, some of them being bound more closely, others more loosely, to the master; but all these people imprint on their own, free, public life the system of life which they have received by association with the master.[27]

Buber's intense admiration for Hasidism did not blind him to its deficiencies. "Hasidism was the one great attempt in the history of the Diaspora . . . to found a true and just community based on religious principles. This attempt failed for a number of reasons, among others because it did not aim for the independence, for the self-determination of the people; or, to state it differently, because its connections with Palestine were only sporadic and not influenced by the desire for national liberation." [28] The true communities that Hasidism established could only be fragmentary realizations of the Jewish ideal when control of the political, economic, and legal dimensions of national existence were not in their own hands.

The Zionism that Buber expressed in later years was inextricably linked to his sense of the Jewish mission. One of his great acts as a representative of Judaism was the open letter he wrote in 1939 in response to Mahatma Gandhi's sharp criticism of Jewish aspirations in Palestine. Where Gandhi had asserted that the Jews searched the

Bible for a sanction that would justify their nationalism, Buber held that the opposite was the case. The Bible confronts Israel with a summons to nationalism by reminding the people of its ancient mission to establish a nation that will embody a God-centered way of life in the very fabric of its social structure. He then refers to a series of biblical commandments that are designed to promote this end. These include: communal ownership of the land; guarantees of the independence of the individual; programs of mutual aid; the sabbath; and even a pattern whereby the social distinctions that continually arise in society might periodically be leveled.[29]

This idealistic pattern of legislation was not thought out by the wise men of the people; the leaders apparently were themselves taken by surprise and overpowered at finding them a part of the convenantal understanding between Israel and God. "No other nation has ever been faced at the beginning of its career with such a mission. Here is something which there is no forgetting and from which there is no release." [30] The individual Jew who appropriates the biblical message must feel its claim upon him, because, as Buber replied to Gandhi:

> At that time we did not carry out that which was imposed upon us; we went into exile with our task unperformed; but the command remained with us, and it has become more urgent than ever. We need our own soil in order to fulfil it: we need the freedom to order our own life: no attempt can be made on foreign soil and under foreign statute. It cannot be that the soil and the freedom for fulfillment are denied us. We are not covetous, Mahatma: our one desire is that at last we may be able to obey.[31]

In *Israel and Palestine* Buber uses every strand of the Jewish tradition—the Bible, the Talmudic epoch, the mysticism of the Kabbalah, the philosophers of medieval Judaism, the great Zaddikim of Hasidism and the modern Zionists—to weave a hymn of praise to the land. He notes that the very structure of the Hebrew language imposes a recognition of the intimate relation of man to the soil. *Adam*, "man," is intimately related to *adamah*, "the earth." Israel cannot fulfill the divine charge until her people are restored to the land.[32]

The land is necessary to the fulfillment of the Jewish mission, but only when it is considered as a challenge and not as a possession. Buber took his cue from such biblical passages as the following one in which God declared: "For the land is mine, for ye are strangers and settlers with me" (Lev 25:23).[33] "This land," Buber comments, "was at no time in the history of Israel simply the property of the people; it was always at the same time a challenge to make of it what God intended to have made of it."[34] And for just this reason it is irreplaceable. Those who regarded Zionism as the answer to anti-Semitism or as a needed stimulus to Jewish creativity might well seek to replace the land of Palestine by Uganda, Madagascar, or other locales whose settlement by the Jewish people might have proved less problematical than their settlement of Palestine. But for Buber and other Jews whose Zionism was grounded in religious convictions, this was unthinkable. "Israel," he said, "would lose its own self if it replaced Palestine by another land and it would lose its own self if it replaced Zion by Palestine."[35]

Because of their conviction that the ideal of Zion must not be subordinated to the political exigencies of a Jewish state, Buber and a number of like-minded men were led into conflict with the leaders of the Jewish settlement in Palestine. And they were led into conflict with the Arabs because of their conviction that Palestine could not be replaced by any other land as the territory on which a Jewish state should be established. They considered the claims of Arabs and Jews to be so different in nature and origin that they could not be objectively pitted against each other to decide which was just and which unjust. Under the name of the *Ichud*, the "Union" party, they advocated the establishment of a bi-national state in which both people could develop the land without either of them imposing its will upon the other.[36]

The proposal of a bi-national state was rejected by both sides, and with the establishment of the State of Israel came the war between Jew and Arab that Buber found even more grievous than the two World Wars. He had hoped that the Jews would exemplify and the Arabs would accept the understanding of the situation that he expressed in the following terms: "The more fertile this soil becomes, the more space there will be for us and for them. We have no desire to dispossess them: we want to live with them. We do not want to dominate them, we want to serve with them." [37]

In 1950 Buber wrote a preface to the English edition of *Israel and Palestine*, which had first appeared in Hebrew in 1944. Although the State of Israel had come into being in the interim he noted that he had not found it necessary to alter any of his text, ". . . which is intended to shed light not on the history of a political enterprise but on that of a religious idea or rather on the spiritual history of a faith." "How much of the latter," he adds, "the political enterprise and its consequences will be able to realize will naturally be revealed only in the course of several generations. But it is only right that, as long as such a spiritual reality lives, history should be responsible to it rather than that it should be responsible to history."[38]

The way to the realization of the ideal of Zion inheres in the uniqueness of Israel as a faith-people. But many Jews retreat from the insecurity of belonging to a unique group that can be readily singled out, and they rush to alter Judaism so that it will fit into classifications that lie at hand among the nations. The radical wing of Reform Judaism sought to rid the faith of the particularity of its national element and to reduce it to the status of a "confession," that is, of a religion in the modern sense of that term.[39] Political Zionism went to the other extreme by throwing off the element of faith in the effort to reduce Israel to the status of a nation among the nations.

> Day by day an increasing number of us are saying: "The period of humanism is past! You cannot swim against the current! Those messianic tidings, the charge of righteousness and justice, was nothing but an expression of our weakness! So come, let us be strong!" Their only wish is to join the wolf pack. . . . Of all the many kinds of assimilation in the course of our history, this is the most terrifying, the most dangerous, this nationalist assimilation. That which we lose on account of it we shall perhaps never acquire again.[40]

Buber's call for a national turning was rejected as an irrelevant idealism by the political leaders of the Jewish settlement in Palestine. While he certainly is a servant of the ideal of Zion, it is important to note that he is not a perfectionist.[41] For one thing, he does not have the antipathy to power that characterizes such perfectionists as the absolute pacifists. "A great historian," he notes, "has asserted that power is evil. But this is not so. Power is intrinsically guiltless; it is the precondition for the actions of man." [42] Power may be used for legitimate or hysterical self-assertion. The latter involves treating the other only as an It, as a means to an end. Legitimate self-assertion affirms the other in his otherness. Buber's attitude toward the Arabs provides an example of legitimate self-assertion. It involved self-assertion because he hoped to use the land of Palestine for Jewish fulfillment. But his love for the land — far from blinding him to the opposing claims of the Arabs — enabled him to appreciate their love for the same land and to seek a resolution that would not involve imposition of one will upon another, but a *modus vivendi* between two peoples.[43]

Another point at which he rejects the council of perfectionism is in his attitude toward force. In his view, even those involved in legitimate forms of self-assertion may have to resort to it. In his letter to Gandhi he dissociated himself from the position Jesus expressed in the Sermon on the Mount, "Do not resist one who is evil" (Mt 5:39), as well as from Gandhi's own position of non-violent resistance.[44]

> For I cannot help withstanding evil when I see that it is about to destroy the good. I am forced to withstand the evil in the world just as the evil within myself. I can only strive not to have to do so by force. I do not want force. But if there is no other way of preventing the evil destroying the good, I trust I shall use force and give myself up into God's hands.[45]

Buber is not a perfectionist, but he is certainly not a relativist: once again he stands on a "narrow ridge." The position he takes may best be grasped by examining his attitude toward compromise. He acknowledges the need for compromise on social issues, but he warns against compromising more than is necessary. "It is true that we are not able to live in perfect justice, and in order to preserve the community of man, we are often compelled to accept wrongs in decisions concerning the community. But what matters is that in every hour of decision we are aware of our responsibility and summon our conscience to weigh exactly how much is necessary to preserve the community, and accept just so much and no more. . . ." [46]

Standing on the "narrow ridge" he sees compromises for what they are and warns against our tendency to imagine that the needs of the hour turn wrong into right. It is of utmost importance that ". . . we do not make a practice of setting aside a certain sphere in which God's command does not hold, but regard those actions as against His command, forced on us by the exigencies of the hour as painful sacrifices; that we do not salve, or let others salve, our conscience when we make decisions concerning public life, but struggle with destiny in fear and trembling lest it burden us with greater guilt than we are compelled to assume." [47]

Confronted with teachings of this character, all too many would say that, while they are most admirable, they cannot be put into effect until frontiers are stabilized and people are secure. Buber uncompromisingly rejects this kind of rationalization, which really involves the view that the end justifies the means. "If the goal to be reached is like the goal which was set, then the nature of the way must be like the goal." [48]

In the modern epoch, when an abstract humanitarianism has emerged to counteract the virulence of fanatical nationalism, the notion of Israel as the "Chosen People," underlying Buber's sense of the Jewish mission, has been a source of embarrassment to those who chafe under the burden of Jewish uniqueness. The first Prime Minister of Israel, David Ben-Gurion, has attempted to preserve the teaching, while palliating its offense, by saying that Israel is indeed a "Chosen People" with a special mission, but so too, are all the other nations. This is only half the truth.

The prophet Amos also knew of the chosenness of all peoples: "Are ye not as the children of the Ethiopians unto me O children of Israel? saith the Lord, Have I not brought up Israel out of the land of Egypt? and the Philistines from Caphtor and Aram from Kir?" (9:7). But there is another verse in Amos in which God declares to Israel: "You only have I known of all the families of the earth, therefore I will visit upon you all your iniquities" (3:2). There is no question here of mere privilege; Israel was summoned to greater responsibility. All nations are chosen, but this does not negate the uniqueness of the divine charge to Israel. "Israel is not a nation like other nations," writes Buber, "no matter how much its representatives have wished it during certain eras. Israel is a people like no other, for it is the only people in the world which, from its earliest beginnings, has been both a nation and a religious community." [49]

Buber has a deep reverence for the Jewish tradition. He warns against its exploitation by those who boast about it without believing in it: those who employ the concept of chosenness without believing in the God who chooses; those who employ the concept of the Chosen People without being willing to assume the burden of fulfilling the prophetic vision of the community of justice and peace.[50] Yet for all the sharpness of Buber's criticisms of the political developments in Israel, he has found there a beginning of creative experiments in communal living that may point mankind a way to genuine community.

One expression of the crisis of our age is the continual enlargement of the units of social organization and the centralization of all activities in the political state, which, by its nature, cannot recognize the concrete person. The state stands in the way of genuine community, which can only grow out of small units whose members can enter into direct relation with one another.[51] The state is necessary for the maintenance of unity within the nation, but it is only valid insofar as it does not destroy the solidarities of the small organic communities within it.[52]

It is in terms of this perspective that Buber sees the creativity of the settlement in Israel. The return to the land on the part of the Haluzim, the "pioneers," was the concrete expression, in work rather than in ideology, of the teachings of a tradition that extended over more than three millennia.[53] They established small village co-operatives and communes, which enabled their members to live in vital relation with one another. Many of them federated into larger units without surrendering their individuality. They sought to exert a creative influence on the national life.

Buber has called these co-operative communities of Israel "an experiment that did not fail." It cannot be said to have succeeded for a number of reasons. There is still much to be desired in the relations within the communities. "A real community," writes Buber, "need not consist of people who are perpetually together; but it must consist of people who, precisely because they are comrades, have mutual access to one another and are ready for one another." [54] Here the image of the early Hasidic communities still governs his vision. Other criticisms follow: the communities have not always had good relations with one another, especially in the matter of mutual help, as the larger ones have failed to encourage smaller struggling units. The influence of all of them on the total life of the nation has still not been as creative as their success within their own communities led Buber to hope it might be. But, in the frank and searching self-criticism of these communities, he sees an element that may enable them to surpass all their previous achievements.[55]

Buber sees no future for capitalism; he has no faith in its ability to achieve economic justice. He is convinced that the nations of the West will be forced into a radical socialization of their economies. He sees two alternatives emerging out of the contemporary crisis. One is the monolithic collectivism of Moscow; "The other," he says, "I would make bold to call Jerusalem." [56]

Jerusalem is an alternative because in Israel there is still a possibility of establishing an organic state, one that is a community of communities. By doing so, the Jewish people would fulfill their age-old mission of pointing the way to a regeneration of humanity, not by means of abstractions such as world government, but as a people of peoples: ". . . a new humanity capable of standing up to the problems of our time can come only from the cooperation of national particularities, not from their being levelled out of existence." [57] Thus Buber reforges, in contemporary terms, "the national universalism of the prophetic faith." [58]

Because he insists that the Jewish mission can be fulfilled

only within the confines of the Jewish State, Buber has been accused of being negative toward Judaism in the Diaspora. His answer is that he is not at all negative to it, but that he cannot help pointing out its fundamental limitation: it can only hope to realize a part of the communal ideal contained in the Jewish mission.[59]

The realization of Jewish life in the Diaspora can, however, be a great one. It is the way pointed to by Hasidism, the way of genuine, though limited, communal expression rooted in the vision of the hallowing of life and the love of God.[60] This realization, though partial, would be the greater part. For to be a people of God Israel must make the two most significant attributes of God revealed to it — the attributes of justice and love — effective in its own life.

> In the Diaspora, it is true, a comprehensive realization of the principle of justice could not be aspired to, since that would have required an autonomous national entity, autonomous national institutions, which could only be hoped for with the return to the Holy Land; but the higher, the decisive principle which alone can knit together the relationship to God and the relationship to man — the principle of love — requires neither organizations nor institutions but can be given effect at any time, at any place.[61]

To show that love is the higher of the two principles, Buber appeals to the fact that man can not be just to God, whereas, he can, and should love God.[62]

No one concerned with Judaism could fail to be stirred by Buber's adaptation of Hasidic piety with its emphasis on love of God. But it is precisely among those who share Buber's concern for the uniqueness of the Jewish mission that we would find the sharpest criticisms of his understanding of Diaspora Judaism. They would regard his view of its possibilities as unduly constricted, because he rejects the authority of the Rabbis to prescribe Jewish practice by means of the Halachah. The dietary and sabbatical laws, to which we have already referred, were only a fraction of the total of the practices it enjoined. In all, the Mitzvoth, the divinely ordained commandments of commission and prohibition, numbered 613, and the Halachic definitions of the precise details of their observance created a countless number of sub-commandments. The elaboration of the Mitzvoth in study and practice were the primary expressions of Jewish separateness, and therefore, of Israel's uniqueness, which Buber has spoken about so eloquently.

To appreciate Buber's negative attitude toward the traditional understanding of the Halachah, we must again recall that, although love of God in and through its injunctions was the underlying ideal, legalism was too often the result. Even Hasidism succumbed to it. In its shift from the effort to infuse the observance of the Mitzvoth with the hallowing intention of fervent faith, to its later phase, in which so many of its adherents must be numbered among the worst exemplars of legalism, Buber sees, ". . . only the old story that in the world of men the shell ever prevails over the kernel." [63] This is one reason he rejects the Hasidic approach to Halachah while passionately affirming its fundamental teaching of the hallowing of the world. And his non-observance of the Mitzvoth is the one reason the contemporary Hasidim have no interest whatsoever in his work on their movement.

The example of Hasidism may have had a strong influence on the development of Buber's attitude toward the Halachah, but it can only be regarded as a contributing factor. The essential element is his conviction that man's response to God cannot be authentic unless it is rooted in the immediacy of dialogical encounter.

In a penetrating discussion of the Ten Commandments he notes that ". . . they are not part of an impersonal codex governing an association of men. They were uttered by an *I* and addressed to a *Thou.*" [64] They cannot be understood apart from the faith situation of encounter, and within that situation no supernatural force compels obedience to them. "Obviously God does not wish to dispense either medals or prison sentences." [65] But since they involve principles, such as the prohibition of murder and theft, which are fundamental to the maintenance of social order, "It is understandable that society does not want to base so vital a matter on so insecure a foundation as faith. . . ." [66] Society removes the commandments from the domain of encounter and converts them into moral absolutes; it moves from "Thou shalt not" to "You must not."

But even moral law is relatively insecure; it can only be enforced by public opinion and the individual may well decide to defy it. Therefore, ". . . the commands and prohibitions are once more transferred, this time to the sphere of 'law,' i.e., they are translated into the language of if-formulations: 'If someone should do this or that, then such and such a thing shall be done to him.' " [67]

Buber sees the presentness and revelatory power of Israel's encounter at Sinai vitiated by this depersonalizing of the divine word and its transformation into a multiplicity of objectively defined laws. However, he regards the process as a necessary one. It is sinful only if society insists on regarding the legal forms into which it has transformed the

Ten Commandments, as the revealed word of Sinai. "But nothing of its vast machinery has anything to do with the situation of the human being who in the midst of personal experience hears and feels himself addressed by the word 'Thou.' " [68]

Since Buber could consistently apply this analysis to the Halachah, it sets him at the opposite pole from the Orthodox who maintain that the entire Torah, Written and Oral, was revealed to Israel at Sinai. They glory in the proliferation of minutiae in the Talmud and in the subsequent stages of the Rabbinic tradition, for they regard them as implicit in the original Mosaic revelation. They insist that there can be no genuine Judaism unless all the Mitzvoth defined by the Halachah are observed; that modifications of any of them leads to the loss of Jewish distinctiveness and, ultimately, to the loss of faith.

Since the emancipation of Jewry from the ghettos, the fabric of Jewish existence has dissolved. To counter this, the Orthodox call for a strengthening of Rabbinic authority that will enable the practice of the Mitzvoth to be enforced once again. Buber disagrees: it is just this authoritarian aspect of the traditional approach to Halachah that produces the destructive abuse of legalism, and this abuse elicits rebellion against Judaism itself. The renewal of Jewish faith and life can only emerge out of the encounters between God and the individual Jew. However much the tradition and the community may help the individual on his way, in the end he can only validly observe those Mitzvoth in which he finds himself addressed as a Thou.

The most illuminationg discussion of Buber's highly individuated approach to the Halachah was initiated by his friend Franz Rosenzweig. On reading a collection of "Lectures on Judaism"[69] that Buber had delivered over the years from 1909 to 1919, Rosenzweig wrote an essay "The Builders," which he addressed to Buber. In this essay he noted that Buber's attitude toward Jewish teachings reflected a remarkable conversion. The early lectures were marked by a radical approach that rejected the main stream of the tradition and affirmed only the "hidden stream" of creative protest, represented, as we have already noted, by the prophets, mystics, heretics, and Zaddikim. In the later lectures Buber urged his hearers to hold themselves open to all Jewish teachings. Until all of them had been studied, the Jew could not say which ones were to be the vehicles of encounters with the eternal Thou.[70]

Rosenzweig noted that, by contrast, Buber's position on the Law, the Halachah, had remained static throughout this series of lectures. He urged Buber to adopt the same position toward Jewish practice that Buber had, in the later lectures, come to take toward Jewish teachings.[71] This, according to Rosenzweig, involved treating the entire range of Mitzvoth, and even the customs that were sanctified by practice, though not formulated by Halachah, as possible vehicles of responsiveness to the divine.[72] But Rosenzweig, in opposition to the Orthodox, held that those that failed to become existentially meaningful, might be discarded by the individual Jew.[73]

In the correspondence with Rosenzweig that followed the appearance of "The Builders," Buber confirmed his opposition to any traditionally oriented approach to Jewish observance.[74] "I do not believe that *revelation* is ever a formulation of law. It is only through man in his self-contradiction that revelation becomes legislation. This is the fact of man."[75]

Rosenzweig insisted that he could not accept revelation as law either. Yet he argued with Buber that just as the words of the Bible confronting one on the printed page may, in the moment of encounter, serve as a medium between man and the divine, so too, by following the prescriptions of the Law, the Jew can hope to find them transformed once again from laws into commandments, from the domain of the "You must," to the domain of "Thou shalt."[76]

To this Buber answered that he was always ready for a given aspect of the Jewish Law to become a commandment. For example, as he grew older and recognized the restlessness of his soul, he increasingly accepted the sabbath, the day of rest. But in opposition to Rosenzweig, Buber insists that he cannot practice any aspect of Jewish Law until it becomes a commandment directly addressed to him by God. In answer, Rosenzweig insisted that the only way to find out which aspects of the Law may become commandments is to put all of them to the test of practice.

Apart from this interchange with Rosenzweig, the most significant consideration of Buber's attitude toward Halachah is one which appeared some thirty-five years later in an extensive essay on "Martin Buber and the Faith of Israel," which was written by Ernst Simon, a friend of both Buber and Rosenzweig, who has adopted the latter's position on this issue. It appeared in an issue of the Hebrew Philosophical Quarterly *Iyyun* that was dedicated to Buber in honor of his eightieth birthday, and in it Simon presents a searching critique of Buber's position on Halachah as well as a passionate appeal for a change in that position.[77] In opposition to Rosenzweig, Simon maintains that there is no great difference between Buber's earlier and later interpretations of Judaism.[78] Simon admits that the details were modified in

Buber's later work, but he insists that even the most recent writings reflect Buber's tendency to oversimplify Judaism by approaching it in terms of radical dichotomies. The later work no longer celebrates the "hidden stream" of creative protest; yet, says Simon, it still isolates those leaders Buber regards as true men of dialogue — the prophets and some of the Zaddikim — from the rest of the leaders of Judaism, such as the priests, the kings, and, especially, from the Rabbis. And Simon claims the Rabbis and the rest preserved Judaism through the ages by concerning themselves with matters of structure and organization — primarily with the Halachah.

Simon presses the implications of this analysis to a point at which his strictures against Buber's approach to the Halachah are more far-reaching than were Rosenzweig's.[79] Simon sees Buber's attitude toward Halachah as a symptom of his tendency to undervalue the role of structure in human affairs, rather than as a peculiar abberation of his approach to Judaism. Simon notes that, while Buber acknowledges the fact that ". . . without It man cannot live. . . . ," he has not paid sufficient attention to the ramifications of this insight. Buber's failure to recognize the creative power of Halachah is a symptom of his excessive preoccupation with the I-Thou relation. Buber does not explore the role of Halachah in enriching the ultimate dimension of the Jewish encounter with God. For example, Buber rejects the Christian affirmation that redemption has transpired in the person of Jesus Christ. In doing so he appeals to the Jewish experience of the unredeemed character of history. Simon agrees with Buber's rejection of the Christian view, but claims that in Buber's case this rejection is almost arbitrary. By attacking the authoritative role of Halachah, Buber attacks the element in the Jewish tradition that stands in sharpest opposition to the Christian claim that redemption has already, in some sense, occurred. Simon holds that the Halachah, by structuring Jewish existence in a God-centered direction, actually comprises a sort of Jewish constitution for the pre-messianic age.[80]

In answer to Simon's criticism, we may recall that in Buber's later writings he does not isolate the prophets and the Zaddikim. He sees their dialogic power as a concentrated form of a power which is to be found throughout Judaism. Furthermore, without the central insights provided by the great men of dialogue, the organizing powers of the other leaders degenerate into sterile institutional forms. The realm of Thou should always be central.

As for Buber's attitude toward Halachah: in Judaism, every aspect of life stands under divine sanction. This is its most creative aspect, provided that the routine that emerges is a reflection of living Torah rather than of rigid laws and codes. In this routine fixed by Halachic definition, Buber, however, sees the threat of an incubus that will cut off the possibility of spontaneous response to the eternal Thou. "I cannot admit the law transformed by man into the realm of my will, if I am to hold myself ready as well for the unmediated word of God directed to a specific hour of life." [81]

His understanding of revelation as encounter, his Zionism, the example of the decline of Hasidism, all contribute to Buber's attitude toward Halachah. It is, as he claims, fearfully difficult to preserve the possibility of spontaneous encounter in the midst of an intricately elaborated religious regime. It is enormously difficult to infuse the performance of the Mitzvoth with the proper intention. Yet this point is not persuasive as a basis for his rejection of their central role in Judaism. The goal he sets the State of Israel is also very difficult, but he does not on that account feel obliged to urge its abandonment.[82]

In view of his differences with Rosenzweig it is interesting to note that years after their correspondence, when criticizing the Pauline position on the Torah, Buber favorably quoted a Talmudic teaching which supports Rosenzweig: the love of God is the only proper motive for the observance of the prescriptions of the Law, but the Jew who cannot observe them for this reason should still observe them — the hope being that if he continues to observe them for the wrong reason, God may grant him the grace to perform them for the right reason.[83] The fact that Buber quotes this teaching against Paul does not necessarily mean that he identifies himself with it, but this Rabbinic teaching is just as relevant to any criticism of his own position.

Simon has also observed the inconsistency implicit in Buber's criticism of Pauline Christianity.[84] Buber, he notes, maintains that Paul was basically in error in his rejection of the Torah. Yet, says Simon, what made Paul's rejection of the Torah so significant was his rejection of the Halachah and this is a rejection which Buber shares, differing only as to the reasons for doing so. Paul rejects the prescriptions of the Halachah as a burden; Buber rejects them because he holds that the Torah is not Law, but the living word of an I-Thou relation. From a Jewish standpoint, this is an extremely truncated version of Torah. Therefore, Simon is convinced that on the issue of Halachah, Rosenzweig has pre-empted Buber's position on the "narrow ridge."

We are now in position to appreciate a singular aspect of Buber's career. Although his outlook is profoundly Jewish, he has, to date, exerted a greater influence on Christian than on Jewish thought.[85] Ernst Simon observed that Buber has been tormented by this anomaly: "How did it happen that Christian theologians understood him better than Jewish leaders or Rabbis?" [86]

The answer is complex, one facet of it involving the tragedy of the Nazi era. In Central Europe, Buber, Rosenzweig, and other Jewish thinkers were pointing the way to a genuine revival of Judaism. Had this community not been destroyed, a generation of Jews with a deep appreciation of his work might have emerged. However, this generation was destroyed, and Buber himself went to Israel where he has exerted little influence. The secular majority of the population reject his religious orientation; the religious elements of the population, who are rigorously Orthodox, reject him because of his non-observance. Both elements have resented his highly critical attitude toward the political behavior, first, of the leaders of the Jewish settlement of Palestine and then, of the State of Israel itself.

But long-range historical factors must also be invoked in explaining the anomaly of his having influenced Christian, particularly Protestant, thinkers to a greater extent than he has influenced those of Judaism. From the seventeenth century Christian theology has tried to mediate between philosophies dominated by the scientific outlook and biblically oriented religion. We have already had occasion to note that Protestantism produced a liberal theology that was responsive to scientific perspectives. In the nineteenth century many of its representatives embraced a "progress" view of history that was grounded in evolutionary thought. They held that the pinnacle of man's spiritual achievement was to be found in the teachings of Jesus Christ, and that these teachings would inevitably come to permeate all societies.

With the outbreak of the First World War the progress view of history received a rude jolt. Protestantism responded to the crisis in terms defined by the New Orthodoxy. Buber's influence on Protestant thought is mainly a function of his appeal to the adherents of this outlook. In reacting against the rationalistic perspective of theological liberalism, they find his religious existentialism, which is to a great extent biblically oriented, an invaluable source of insights.

On the other hand, the rise of science made little impact on Judaism because of the cultural isolation imposed by the ghettos. At the beginning of the nineteenth century the process of the emancipation of Jewry from the ghettos began in France, and, in the course of that century, it spread throughout Europe. Among the Jews who took advantage of the new freedom and plunged themselves into modern culture there were many who converted to Christianity; but the others, who were attached to their Jewish heritage, fought to preserve it. They summarily rejected the rigidity of Orthodoxy, and, in their efforts to attain a new understanding of Judaism, moved from the medieval to the modern world in one stride. It is no wonder that they adopted the rationalistic perspectives of liberal theology with the ardor of recent converts. The evolutionary thinking that had influenced liberal Protestant thought was especially appealing since it promised steady and inevitable progress toward the Messianic Age, when the persecutions that had characterized so much of Jewish history would be permanently at an end.

As Judaism, by force of historical circumstances, was late

in developing a modern religious outlook, so too, it has been late in deserting some of the more naïve formulations associated with nineteenth-century modernism. Furthermore, there is among Jews a natural tendency to associate liberalism in all its forms—political, cultural, and religious—with the emancipation of Jewry from the ghettos. The religious liberals of Judaism, have therefore been reluctant to modify their outlook and have been very suspicious of the New Orthodoxy, which has gained such wide influence in Protestant circles. They have been afraid that it presages a reactionary trend despite the fact that many of its outstanding representatives, thinkers like Reinhold Niebuhr and Paul Tillich, have, politically, been outstanding liberals. Because Buber is an existentialist who is highly critical of liberal theology, this suspicion extends to him and mitigates the influence he might have exerted on the liberal thinkers of Reformed and Conservative Judaism. On the other hand, the mere fact that he is not an observant Jew is enough to prevent his having influence on Orthodox circles outside of Israel as well as on those within it.

Finally, the active character of Jewish religion, its concern with deed, that is, with Mitzvoth, has meant that all forms of organized Judaism in the modern world have devoted a major part of their attention to questions of observance. The Orthodox have been concerned with holding the line, the Reformed and Conservative movements with the question of just where to draw the new lines. Buber has had little to say about this sort of question. He has been negative in his personal approach to questions of Jewish observance, but, because he has never expressed his views in terms of a "program," he has had little relevance to this practical concern of religious Jewry.

Yet Buber's influence on Jewish religious circles has, despite all these factors, increased since the Second World War, and there are indications that it will continue to grow. It may increase among liberals because the forces that have led Protestant thinkers to become critical of liberal theology will probably modify the outlook of liberal Jewish thinkers. To some extent, this is already happening. His influence may increase among the Orthodox because Judaism in America is producing a form of Orthodoxy that is responsive to modern culture. In this situation, Buber could prove to be an effective mediator.

There is no question of his earnest desire to see a turning to God within the congregations of Judaism:

> My heart is at one with those among Israel who today, equally distant from blind traditionalism and blind contradictoriness, strive with a striving meant to precede a renewal of the forms of both faith and life.[87]

7. The Jewish Jesus and The Christ of Faith

> From my youth onwards I have found in Jesus my great brother. That Christianity has regarded and does regard him as God and Savior has always appeared to me a fact of the highest importance which, for his sake and my own, I must endeavor to understand. . . . My own fraternally open relationship to him has grown ever stronger and clearer, and today [1950] I see him more strongly and clearly than ever before.
>
> I am more than ever certain that a great place belongs to him in Israel's history of faith and that this place cannot be described by any of the usual categories.[1]

This is Martin Buber's most eloquent statement of his intense involvement with the character of Jesus of Nazareth, but there are many other texts which witness to it. In *I and Thou* he cited Goethe as the man who most fully realized the I-Thou relation with the realm of nature; Socrates as the one who best exemplified the relation between man and man; and he selected Jesus to illustrate the deepest realization of the relation between man and the eternal Thou: ". . . how powerful, even to being overpowering, and how legitimate, even to being self-evident, is the saying of I by Jesus! For it is the I of the unconditional relation in which the man calls his Thou Father in such a way that he himself is simply Son, and nothing else but Son."[2]

Buber's "fraternally open relationship" to Jesus has been a source of confusion to some readers, both Christian and Jewish, who conclude that he is a Christian in all but the name. Ronald Gregor Smith, translator into English of *I and Thou* and other important writings of Buber, has written an essay on "The Religion of Martin Buber," which tries to show that at "the deeper level," Buber may in some sense be considered a Christian.[3] If this deeper level is in any way related to the normal use of "Christian" as a religious designation, nothing could be further from the truth. It is because of his sense of knowing Jesus from within, ". . . in the impulses and stirrings of his [Jesus'] Jewish being. . . .", that Buber has emerged as one of the most trenchant critics of the understanding of Jesus as the "Christ of Faith," the central figure of trinitarian Christianity.[4]

In *Two Types of Faith,* an extensive work representing the fruits of his lifetime of New Testament study, Buber tries, in effect, to reclaim the figure of Jesus for Judaism. In doing so, Buber does not approach the teachings of Christianity from the standpoint of their truth or falsity. When he deals with Jesus, he does not ask whether or not Jesus actually arose from the dead; when he presents the teachings of Paul, he does not ask whether they were or were not initiated in supernatural fashion by an encounter with the risen Christ. He is concerned with analyzing the contents of the New Testament against the background of the Jewish Bible and of Pharasaic Judaism, and with pointing to the similarities and differences in the views of God and man, of creation and redemption that arise among them.

That he regards the Jewish Bible as the most authentic expression of the relation between God and man emerges on every page. Yet it must certainly be noted that there can be no question of objective knowledge or of proofs that validate the teachings of the one faith or the other. At the outset, Buber explicitly acknowledges the fact that he can have no access to those Christian insights that can come only to the believer living in the situation of faith.[5]

Buber's approach to Jesus must be taken within the context of his understanding of messianism, especially in connection with his view of the shift from the mysterious, but emphatically prophetic, message of the Second Isaiah to the apocalyptic view of the book of Daniel and the Inter-Testamental literature. We may recall his presentation of the "Servant" passages as referring to a line of prophets who witness to the divine will by proclamation, through their suffering, and even through martyrdom, but who nevertheless remain "arrows concealed in the divine quiver." They make no public messianic claims.

Elaborating a position that was suggested to him by the work of Albert Schweitzer, Buber sees Jesus as teaching and working within the shadow of the Servant.[6] At a crucial moment in his career — the one recorded in the form of an interchange with Peter: "Whom say ye that I am?" "Thou art the Christ, the son of the living God!" (Mt 16:15, 16) — he becomes conscious of himself as being the one awaited by the centuries. At this point, Buber observes, he steps out of the quiver and declares himself the Messiah, but here Jesus uses the term in the prophetic sense. At his trial, the moment of crisis, Jesus moves from the this-worldly frame of reference of the prophetic tradition of the Servant to the otherworldly messianism of the book of

Daniel with its talk of the Son of Man riding on a cloud. In other words, in the trial scene Buber finds a shift in the self-consciousness of Jesus, who moves from a prophetic self-understanding in terms of human fulfillment to an apocalyptic image of the Savior descending from above.[7]

Although he is sure that Jesus deserves a special place in the messianic development of Israel's faith, Buber is convinced that Judaism will never recognize Jesus as the Messiah. There is unquestionably an unbridgeable gap between Judaism and Christianity at this point. But if Buber sees Jesus as a great figure within the history of Jewish messianism, without recognizing him as the Messiah, we may well wonder what role, "not to be described by any of the usual categories," he actually assigns to him. The answer is clear. He regards Jesus as a Servant of the Lord who, had he remained concealed in the divine quiver, would have stood in the prophetic line of the Servants that was announced by Deutero-Isaiah. Since he did not do so, he became the initiator of the series of false messiahs, which culminated in Sabbatai Zevi.

> Whatever meaning the appearance of Jesus bore for the Gentiles . . . as seen from the point of view of Judaism, Jesus is the first in the series of men who acknowledged to themselves in their souls and openly in their words their messiahship and thus stepped out of the seclusion of the servants of God, which is the real "messianic secret." That this First One . . . was incomparably the purest, most rightful of them all, the one most endowed with real messianic power, does not alter the fact that he was the first, yea, it belongs rather to it, belongs to that awful and pathetic character of reality which clings to the whole messianic series.[8]

Shifting our attention from the person to the teachings of Jesus, we find that Buber regards them as thoroughly Jewish. As he translates it, Jesus, in his initial proclamation declares: "The appointed time is fulfilled and God's rule has come near. Turn and believe in (or trust) the message" (Mk 1:15). The notion of fulfilled time sets history within a cosmic framework. God is, as always in Judaism, providentially concerned with the doings of man in the concrete hour. The reference to God's rule reminds his listeners of the covenant at Sinai in which God was accepted as the ruler of Israel. The call for the turning sets Jesus directly in the line of the prophets.[9] Together, the three principles constitute ". . . an heirloom of the religiosity of Israel. . . ."[10] The trust demanded is the "standing fast" in the midst of historical trials that shake one's faith. It is the fidelity that responds to the faithfulness of God, ". . . only if you stand firm in the fundamental relationship of your life do you have an essential stability."[11] This is the teaching that Jesus inherits from the message of the first Isaiah who counseled the king and the people to stand firm in their faith in God and not to rely on alliances with Assyria to protect them from their neighbors.

In the Sermon on the Mount, Jesus also stands within Judaism, though at an extreme end of its spectrum.[12] He stands in the ranks of Jewish leaders who have sharply criticized the waywardness of the people; but so do the very Pharisees who are presented as his bitter opponents. The Pharisees demand that the people fulfill the terms of the covenant at Sinai by performing the Mitzvoth, the sacred commandments, with the full intention of the heart. Nevertheless, Jesus opposed them because he believed that the appointed time was fulfilled. Out of an urgency born of the approaching end of the aeon, he attempted to break through the form of the Torah as it had been ordained at Sinai and to penetrate directly into the divine intention itself. Hence his severity on the matter of divorce, which he said Moses permitted only because of the people's "hardness of heart." [13] His sense of the impending end of history also explains the perfectionism of the demand to "resist not the evil," another teaching that set him in opposition to the Pharisees. The Pharisees were not Zealots advocating the overthrow of the Romans by armed rebellion. They rejected this movement and its policies, but they opposed evil with their own spiritual methods and could not renounce resistance to evil out of hand.[14]

The differences between Jesus and the Pharisees were differences of degree. Standing in the same fundamental faith relation, he sharpened the divine demands. This is particularly apparent in his demand that men love their enemies. At this point he definitely steps beyond the Pharisees, who taught that men must love the companions they meet on life's way and thereby come to love God, but who could not imagine that men ought to love the enemies of God, the men who deny their creator.[15]

> All in all, the saying of Jesus about love for the enemy derives its light from the world of Judaism in which he stands and which he seems to contest; and he outshines it. It is indeed always so when a person in the sign of the *Kairos* [fulfillment of time in the eschatological sense] demands the impossible in such a way that he compels men to will the possible more strongly than before. But one should not fail to appreciate the bearers of the plain light below from amongst whom he arose: those who enjoined much that was possible so as

> not to cause men to despair of being able to serve God in their poor everyday affairs.[16]

It is fascinating to note that Buber here reverses the Christian interpretation, initiated by Paul, of the relation between the work of Jesus and that of the Pharisees. Paul saw the Pharisees as endlessly multiplying regulations, thereby increasing the burden of the people who could not fulfill the many prescriptions of the "Law"; Buber, in line with the Jewish tradition, sees the Pharisees as decreasing the burden of the people by adapting the Torah to the specific situations of everyday life. Paul sees Jesus as releasing the Jews from the yoke of the "Law" by bringing them to God through faith in himself. Buber sees Jesus as demanding perfection of men. Since the end Jesus anticipated did not occur and men must still live in history, this demand, Buber holds, can only increase the burden of their existence by driving men to despair at their failure to fulfill it.

Finally, Buber points to one of Jesus' sayings, which, he is convinced, was meant to ward off the very interpretation of his life and work that, despite this warning, became the basis of Christianity: "Why callest thou me good? There is none good but God alone" (Mk 10:18). In this statement Buber sees the great line of the Old Testament teaching of the non-humanity of God and the non-divinity of man. "No theological interpretation can weaken the directness of this statement."[17] That nevertheless Christianity did deify Jesus is attributable in large measure to the work of one whom Buber regards as a religious genius, but a dark one, Saul of Tarsus, known to the generations of believers as Saint Paul.

In Paul, Buber sees a gigantic figure who is the real originator of the Christian conception of faith.[18] Paul uses the figure of Jesus Christ to bring the God of Israel to the nations. In doing so, however, he steps outside the faith situation of the Jewish Bible. As a result, the Jesus he brings to the nations fails to fulfill the ancient mission of Israel: to lead mankind to genuine humanity by establishing a nation in justice and peace.

In the Jewish Bible Buber finds the God of power, but also the God of love. He is the creator, but He is also the one who becomes immediately present to man in encounter. This presence witnesses, even in the midst of historical disasters, to the ultimately redemptive character of His activity. It also assures men that despite His power, which stands beyond the world and beyond imagination, men need no mediator to the divine. They can approach Him with the full love of their hearts, their souls, their might. Buber also finds in the Jewish Bible the central teaching we have considered so often: man — created in the image of God with the power of obedience and disobedience to the divine will — is summoned to the turning.

Buber insists that in the thought of Paul all this has changed. God, who for Jesus was still the Father known in the immediacy of encounter, has now become the remote God of apocalyptic literature. Paul's God has placed this aeon (the one that Christ's appearance was supposed to have brought to its end) in the hands of other powers.[19] "Contrary to the Old Testament * Paul's God," says Buber, "does not have regard for the people to whom He speaks out of the cloud, or rather causes His angels to speak." [20] This God simply uses generations of men as means for

* As we have noted, Buber rejects the use of the name the "Old Testament" and calls it the "Jewish" or "Hebrew" Bible, but in this work, which contrasts the "Old" with the "New," Buber continually uses the term "Old Testament."

the fulfillment of His plan. Paul's view of this plan could only have been persuasive in the atmosphere of the Hellenistic world whose pessimism gave full scope to Persian dualism with its catastrophic struggles between the powers of good and evil.

Paul held that man was created by God with a law in his body that opposes the law in his reason, that is, the law in his spirit that would obey the divine will. Here we have the central teaching of dualism: man as a creature of two separate warring natures. The law in man's body enables Satan to entice man in sin.[21] Then follows the process whereby man is hardened in his sin; this is effected by "the powers" into whose hands God has committed the administration of the cosmic epoch between the creation of man and the coming of Jesus Christ.[22]

As Buber understands Paul's view, not only did God, in His initial act of creation, impart a fatal flaw to man in the form of the rebellious law embedded in human flesh, He even drove man deeper into sin in His act of revelation. Paul, regarding the Torah in terms of the burden of the "Law," claimed that far from having been the greatest gift given by God to Israel, the Torah, by specifying all sorts of commandments and prohibitions, goaded Israel into further sinfulness.[23] This pattern of divine commandment and human sinning persisted, because, until the coming of Jesus Christ, there was no power that could release men from their bondage to the sinful impulses to which they were enslaved through the fall of Adam. In Paul's scheme, God Himself, ". . . apparently entirely apart from Christ, makes those once chosen by Him unfree in order to be able to set them free by Christ, He makes them deserving of wrath in order to deliver them from wrath."[24]

Since the wrath of God accumulates throughout the generations of man without any generation having been virtuous enough to mollify Him, ". . . God's sense of justice," Buber notes, "inexorably demands the appropriate, i.e. measureless, punishment for the 'sin which is sinful beyond measure.' " Men are finite creatures in bondage to sin and, therefore, Paul holds that, "Only God Himself can effect the propitiation of an infinite guilt, by making His Son, the Christ, take the atoning suffering upon himself, so that all who believe in Christ are saved through him. . . . The prophetic idea of the man who suffers for God's sake has here given way to that of God who suffers for the sake of man." [25]

Reflecting on this apocalyptic vision of God and His plan, Buber says, "When I contemplate this God I no longer recognize the God of Jesus, nor his world in this world of Paul's." [26] For the God of Jesus was the God of the Jewish Bible and the world of Jesus was the world of the Pharisees.

Nor does Buber conclude his argument here. He notes that the Jewish Bible knows of God's wrath just as much as Paul's Letters know of it, but in the Jewish Bible His wrath is always a fatherly anger directed against a disobedient child. Even when wrathful the God of the Jewish Bible does not want to withdraw His love. The anthropomorphisms with which the Jewish Bible abounds preserve the crucial dialogical reality, the sense of direct personal relatedness. If Israel, says Buber, knows of that other Pauline theme, the evil powers, it does not know about, ". . . one which, for longer than the purpose of temptation, was allowed to rule in God's stead; never, not even in the most deadly act of requital by God, is the bond of immediacy broken." [27] Far from seeing the entire epoch from the fall of Adam to the appearance of Jesus Christ as one in which a remote God has left the world in the hands of the powers of darkness, "To Pharasaic Judaism the creation of man and the revelation are works of the divine love." [28]

Buber maintains that Israel always knew that it was to hallow the basic drives and institutions that comprise the materials of human existence. Hunger, sex, the will to power, politics, economics, and geographical location — all these taken together constitute the material with which man must relate himself to God.[29] In Paul's dualism, which sets the law of the body in opposition to the law of the mind, and the earthly in opposition to the spiritual, Buber sees a calamitous sundering of this organic faith of Israel which was rooted in the fullness of the life of a people as lived on the land. The very term used to describe the Christian community, "The Israel of the *Spirit*" witnesses to the effectiveness of the Pauline alteration.

Paul used an organic image to describe the church; he called it the "body" of which Christ was the "head," the "members" being, therefore, inextricably linked to each other and to that head. But this striking metaphor could not alter the fact that, in comparison with the "Old Israel," the Church was an artificial community without organic roots. Just as the Jews in the Diaspora could not establish genuine community because its members lacked control over their national environment, the Church, according to Buber, could not become a genuine community because it was not created out of organic local communities.[30] In their local settings its people identified themselves as French, English, or even more narrowly, according to their loyalties to province or town.

> Paul often speaks about Jews and Greeks, but never in connexion with the reality of their nationalities: he is only concerned with the newly-established community, which by its nature is not a nation. The conception of the "holy nation" in its strict sense has faded altogether, it does not enter into the consciousness of Christendom, and soon that of the Church takes its place. The consequence of all this is that even in the mass-baptisms of the West . . . the individuals as individuals, not the nations, became Christian, that is, subject to Christ: the "People of God" was Christendom, which in its nature differed from the nations, and these remain in their own nature and their own law as they were.[31]

Here Buber finds the root of the great rift within medieval Christendom; the rift between members of the religious orders who fulfilled the demands of the Church and lived a life of withdrawn and ascetic holiness and those who lived the normal life of their times. Neither group hallowed the elemental aspects of life. Bringing marriage and other activities within the sacramental system of the Church did not alter the Christian ideal: the individual who achieves the status of a saint by overcoming his natural drives. Paul recommended marriage only if people were incapable, because of the needs of the flesh, of adopting his own practice of celibacy.

In comparing the faith of Israel with that of the Church, Buber finds this same contrast between the organic and the artificial. The faith of Israel, as expressed in the Jewish Bible, involves the relation of trust in God and in His purposes. There are many reasons that can be offered to justify this trust, and in the moments of His hiddenness they are all advanced. But in the end, the reasons are not sufficient to justify the trust; if they were, we would not be dealing with faith at all.[32]

There is another, indeed Buber claims, only one other, type of faith: accepting something as true without being able to offer sufficient reasons for doing so. This type of faith is of Greek origin and is based upon philosophical illumination, where one suddenly sees that which had always been true. While these two types of faith are not mutually exclusive, and are rarely to be found in their pure forms, Buber sees early Christianity exemplifying faith as acceptance of truth to the same degree that the Jewish Bible exemplifies faith as the relation of trust.[33]

It is obvious that the Christian community, and particularly those members of it who had known Jesus during his ministry, trusted him in a personal way. But the conviction that he was, as Messiah, the only Son of God, and that he had power to save, exemplified the second type of faith. It could only be accepted as true when one moved behind the human appearance to the supra-human reality. In the case of those who had not known Jesus "after the flesh," the situation was even clearer; they had to move from the teaching of Jesus as mediated by the preaching of the Apostles to accepting the truth of the resurrection and the implications that were drawn from it. Only in this way could divine power be welded to the manifest goodness of the man Jesus of Nazareth. As we shift from the faith of Jesus himself, which is the clearest instance of trust in the person of the heavenly Father, to Paul's faith that his risen Lord is sitting at the right hand of God, we move from trust to belief.[34]

The work of Paul in converting the Jewish Bible's trust in God into the central belief that certain things were true of Jesus of Nazareth was carried further by the Gospel of

John and completed by the work of the theologians. They substituted the image of Christ for the imageless God of Judaism and produced the dogma of the Council of Chalcedon (held in 451), which declared that Jesus Christ, the second person of the Trinity, had a complete divine and a complete human nature mysteriously united in him.[35] Buber regards this development as a process of deification that sundered the expressions of faith from the immediacy of encounters with God, whereas, "reverence for the absolute without the use of an intermediate agency is the principle of Israel's everlasting life."[36]

The faith of Israel must be expressed in terms of paradoxes, but we have noted that, as Buber presents them, they derive from direct relation between man and God — from the sense of His nearness and His hiddenness, His power and His love. The individual, born into the organic community of Judaism, does not need to change his way of looking at the world in order to apprehend the meaning of these paradoxical expressions of faith. He has to prove his faith true in an existential sense by persevering in his trustful relation to God.

Buber regards the paradoxes used in expounding the Christian Faith as extreme, because Christianity's fundamental affirmation bridges the unbridgeable, namely, the gulf between divine and human being. All the brilliance of centuries of Christian theology has been devoted to explicating conceivable meanings for the trinitarian formulations of the unity of God despite the threefold character of the divine Person, and for the unity of Christ in spite of his twofold, divine and human, nature. Whatever riches the Christian life of devotion may offer to the initiated who have entered its sanctuary, in the forecourt Buber sees a leap of faith by which the individual convert must accept as true something that he has hitherto regarded as absurd. There is no other entrance.[37] Reflecting on the process that led away from the Jewish faith of Jesus himself to the dogmatic formulations of trinitarian Christianity, Buber notes a gain and a loss.

> The gain was the most sublime of all theologies; it was procured at the expense of the plain, concrete and situation-bound dialogicism of the original man of the Bible, who found eternity, not in the super-temporal spirit, but in the depth of the actual moment. The Jesus of the genuine tradition still belongs to that, but the Jesus of theology does so no longer.[38]

Paul's shift from the world-affirming faith of the Jewish Bible to the apocalyptic world-view, which denies the possibility of redemption in history, was naturally reflected in his understanding of man. His basic pessimism led him to the denial of the most fundamental possibility known to the Jewish Bible, the possibility of the turning. This possibility was maintained by Judaism throughout the centuries of the biblical epoch and in the many centuries of the Diaspora, despite the familiarity of Jewish leaders with the waywardness of man and the evil inclinations of his heart. "The deprecation of man," Buber declares, "is foreign to genuine Judaism." [39]

The divine plan detailed by Paul was one that drained men of their capacity for free response to the challenges of life and history. He initiated the doctrine of "original sin," which, as Buber understands it, holds that the fall of Adam into sin necessarily enslaved the future generations of man to it.[40] Against this doctrine Buber sets the teaching of the turning: provided the individual exerts his whole being in the effort to accomplish it, he is not prevented by anything, not even by the sin of the first man. Man sins as Adam sinned and not because Adam sinned.[41]

The famous Pauline teaching of "justification by faith" is only to be understood as a corollary of his doctrine of sin. Paul sees sin as a form of quicksand; man's efforts to extricate himself only serve to ensnare him further. His hope for salvation does not rest on the possibility of turning or on any other action of his own. Salvation comes only through his belief in Jesus Christ as Lord and Savior. This belief must itself be granted the individual by grace, that is, as an unmerited gift from the merciful God to the unworthy sinner. Men, whom the divine justice would unqualifiedly condemn because of their involvement in the curse of Adam, are justified before Him by the merciful gift of belief in Jesus Christ, ". . . in redeeming the world by the surrender of His son God redeems Himself from the fate of His justice, which would condemn it."[42]

In the Old Testament the Torah was understood as instruction that a man was capable of carrying out: "For the word is very nigh to thee, in thy mouth and in thy heart, to do it" (Deut 30:14). Buber notes that Paul reads his doctrine of justification by faith back into the Old Testament by eliminating the crucial words "to do it" when he quotes this verse. And Paul interprets the word that is near to the human heart as belief in Jesus Christ as the risen Lord.[43] "To be sure, so Paul thinks, as the will of God the Torah must be fulfilled; but its purpose is to cause man to whom it is given to be frustrated precisely by this imperative, so that he might submit to grace."[44] This not only contradicts the Jewish Bible, but it also contradicts the teaching of

Jesus, whose first words, we may recall, involved an appeal for the turning.

Generations of Christian theologians have agreed with Paul in rejecting the Jewish understanding of the turning. "Some time ago," Buber notes, "a Catholic theologian saw in this conception a 'Jewish activism' to which grace is unknown. But it is not so. We are not the less serious about grace because we are serious about the human power of deciding, and through decision the soul finds a way which will lead it to grace." [45]

Buber and the Christian theologians clearly mean different things by the term grace. The theologians see it as the divine gift of belief in the redemptive power of Jesus Christ, and the power to goodness which derives from it; Buber regards it as the manifestation of divine power which confirms the human decision for God.[46] This is the basis of his declaration that, "We have to be concerned, to be troubled, not about the other side but about our own side, not about grace but about will." [47] If a man turns to God and acts with the full intention of faith, he can trust God's gracious response, ". . . it is senseless to ask how far my action reaches and where God's grace begins; there is no common border-line; what concerns me alone, before I bring something about, is my action, and what concerns me alone, when the action is successfully done, is God's grace." [48]

We should remember that Buber offers no objective demonstrations for paradoxes, they are born of his immediate experience.

> Not once only in his life was man free to choose or reject God, or rather, to leave Him unchosen, man is always free to do this or that. Does that mean

> that God has given away one particle of His power to determine the course of events? We only ask that question, when we are busy subsuming God under our logical categories. In the moments when we break through we have an immediate experience of our freedom, and yet in these moments we also know by an immediate experience that God's hand has carried us.[49]

Because its pessimism regarding the capacity of the human will to turn dissolves the reality of that mystery that is central to the faith of Israel — man as an independent partner of God in the work of redemption — Buber sees Paulinism as a debility of the spirit to which Christianity is periodically prone. By separating God's love from His creative activity, by separating holiness from the everyday life of ordinary men, by individualizing the religious impulse, Pauline thinking contributes to that emasculation of the spirit in which religion occupies only a special domain of life.[50]

Buber's view of the thought of Paul, and of its influence on Christian theology, is based on rigorous scholarship and is valid in the sense that he is able to cite evidence to support his conclusions. His view of Paul is, however, extremely one-sided. Paul was a man of many tensions. Not only was there a "law in his body" that opposed the "law of his reason," there was a Hebraism in his thinking that struggled with his Hellenistic dualism. The Hebraic side is the one Buber neglects.

This is not the place to enter into the technical disputes that rage around Pauline terminology. For example, the scholars differ regarding the nuances of the terms "flesh" and "body" as they appear in his Letters. Some interpreters insist that close examination shows that, for the most part, Paul did not identify the sinful impulse in man with the body, as dualists do, but with the "flesh" as standing for the excessive self-assertiveness of the individual, a self-assertiveness that separates him from God.[51] This latter position is not alien to the understanding of sin in the Jewish Bible.

In tension with Paul's apocalyptic preoccupation with the divine plan of salvation, a plan that Buber is right in seeing as one that empties history of all meaning, there stands Paul's sense of the inner conflict of the self striving toward salvation — a conflict which is by no means empty of significance. Far from involving the one-sided derogation of the will described in *Two Types of Faith*, it involves a paradoxical affirmation of the power and limitations of the will: ". . . work out your salvation with fear and trembling for it is God who worketh in you both to will and to do" (Phil 2:12, 13). This is not fundamentally different from Buber's statement that, "In the moments when we break through we have an immediate experience of our freedom, and yet in these moments we also know by an immediate experience that God's hand has carried us."

We have noted that Buber's approach to the Jewish Bible is highly selective. This is no less true of his approach to the Christian one. In dealing with Jesus he concentrates upon those teachings in which Jesus summons men to the turning and ignores those teachings in which Jesus expresses a pessimism that is akin to Paul's, as in Jesus' denunication of the "generation of vipers" and his emphasis on the narrowness of the gate that leads to salvation as contrasted with the broadness of the one that leads to damnation. This pessimism is most in evidence in that central paradox that we have already alluded to, "whosoever shall seek to save his life shall lose it; and whosoever shall lose his life shall preserve it" (Lk 17:33). Here the capacity of man to achieve salvation through the exertions of his will is called into question. Jesus implies that divine grace is needed in order to prevent the individual's seeking of God from becoming a form of self-seeking. In the very process of trying to rid himself of excessive self-concern the individual may intensify it.

There are many other points where Paul stands closer to the Jesus of the first three Gospels than any reader of Buber's *Two Types of Faith* would imagine. Paul emphasizes man's bondage to sin in order to condemn self-righteousness; he does not do so in order to decry man. As Jesus rebuked men for noticing the splinter in their neighbor's eye while missing the log in their own and warned them to judge not that they be not judged, so Paul said: "Therefore, thou are inexcusable, O man, whosoever thou art that judgest: for wherein thou judgest another, thou condemnest thyself; for thou that judgest doest the same things" (Rom 2:1).

Buber also neglects the celebration of joy in "the new life" that runs through the Pauline Letters. Paul's celebration of the "new creation," which takes place in the individual who accepts Jesus as his Lord and Savior, may lack the earthy exuberance of the parable of the Prodigal Son, but it preserves the note of glad tidings that is central to the Gospel.

Buber's reading of Paul may omit a great deal, but what he does report about Paul is really to be found in the Letters. In the current revival of Pauline thinking in Christian circles Buber sees a symptom of the sickness of our age. Although ostensibly concerned with liberating the self from excessive self-preoccupation, it encourages the wrong kind of inwardness by focusing so intensely upon sin. It involves the self in a concern for the state of its soul that is rather like a continual taking of its "spiritual temperature."

In *The Way of Man*, a short book that is his most effective presentation of Hasidic teachings, Buber provides a striking contrast to this type of spirituality.[52] He titles one chapter "Beginning With Oneself," and the following one "Not to be Preoccupied With Oneself." [53] He resolves the apparent conflict by noting that the first injunction is to *begin* with oneself. "To begin with oneself, but not to end with oneself; to start from oneself, but not to aim at oneself; to comprehend oneself, but not to be preoccupied with oneself." [54] A Zaddik told a colleague who was brooding about the fact that he had come to an advanced age without having achieved true repentance, ". . . you are thinking only of yourself. How about forgetting yourself and thinking of the world?" [55]

Buber's understanding of the deleterious effects of Pauline thinking upon its adherents derives, in large measure, from the impact the emphatically Pauline outlook of Kierkegaard made upon him. But before we consider Buber's specific criticisms of Kierkegaard, it will be helpful to consider some of the philosophical differences that underlie the religious existentialism of these two thinkers.

Despite his insistence upon dealing with the concrete individual, Kierkegaard's approach to God is abstract and derived from Christian dogma. He begins with the problematics of theology rather than with the encounters of faith. With unrelieved intensity, he focuses on pairs of opposites which he defines with philosophical precision — infinite and finite, eternal and temporal, necessity and freedom — and then declares that the individual, in order to come to faith, must make the leap whereby he sees these opposites united in Jesus Christ. Indeed, Jesus Christ unites in himself the opposites that, in the view of Judaism throughout the ages, can never be united: divinity and humanity.

The leap can only be made by embracing the absurdity involved, that is, by staking one's destiny on the proposition that the eternal, which stands by definition utterly apart from time, entered time and history in the form of an existing individual. In Kierkegaard's terms, the problem of Christianity is that, "The eternal happiness of the individual is decided in time through the relationship to something historical, which is furthermore of such a character as to include in its composition that which by virtue of its essence cannot become historical, and must therefore become such by virtue of an absurdity." [56]

The absurdity of the leap is somewhat mitigated by the fact that Kierkegaard's analysis of the Christian Faith is set in counterpoint to his analysis of selfhood. Man lives in time, yet with an awareness of eternity; he is personally limited, yet to become a self, he must, in freedom, explore the limitless character of his potentialities. Therefore, the achievement of authentic selfhood involves grounding the self in the absolute; this means sustaining the tension of these opposites within the self and seeing them in relation to Jesus Christ in whom they are already combined in a way that manifests their ultimate significance.

Linking the analysis of Christian Faith to the analysis of selfhood may mitigate the absurdity involved in Kierkegaard's leap of faith, but it does not mitigate its utterly forced character, because the self that Kierkegaard analyzes is the individual standing alone before God. Buber's criticisms of Kierkegaard probe this view of the isolated self which was so intimately linked to Kierkegaard's biography.

Kierkegaard broke his engagement to Regina Olsen on the grounds that any deep attachment to a finite good would weaken his essential relation to the absolute. In order to devote himself to God he felt that he had to turn away from all earthly objects of love. But Buber insists:

> That is sublimely to misunderstand God. Creation is not a hurdle on the road to God, it is the road itself. We are created along with one another and directed to a life with one another. Creatures are placed in my way so that I, their fellow-creature, by means of them and with them find the way to God. A God reached by exclusion would not be the God of all lives in whom all life is fulfilled. . . . God wants us to come to Him by means of the Reginas he has created and not by renunciation of them.[57]

By setting man an "either/or" choice between God and His creation, Kierkegaard succumbs to a dualism that sees the force of evil as so radical that the world can no longer be identified with that creation which God proclaimed as being so "very good" (Gen 1:31). Kierkegaard saw other men as obstacles to the isolated individual in his search for salvation rather than companions on the way. Buber also knows that the individual must prove his faith with his own life, but as a Jew he knows how greatly the community may help the individual in this test. "What is decisive is that I relate myself to the divine as to Being which is over against me, though *not* over against me *alone.*" [58] The point may best be summarized by means of a statement in which Buber not only expresses his fundamental criticism of Kierkegaard's view of the isolated individual, but in which he indicates the source of his criticism. "One must have essential intercourse only with God, says Kierkegaard. It is impossible, says Hasidism, to have truly essential intercourse with God when there is no essential intercourse with men." [59]

Reading Kierkegaard's *Journals*, as well as the books he wrote around the time he broke off his engagement, we see how pitiful his situation was. He simply could not "let go" of himself to recognize Regina as a "Thou." Possessed by a self-absorption that was demonic in its intensity, he continually used his relation with her to measure the state of his soul. Here, if ever, there was a man who needed to heed the injunction to stop thinking of himself and to think of the world. And Buber certainly had Kierkegaard in mind when he wrote that, "Meeting with God does not come to man in order that he may concern himself with God, but in order that he may confirm that there is meaning in the world." [60]

This presentation of Kierkegaard has not done justice to the originality and power of his existentialism and to the penetration of his psychological insights. It could not develop the sense in which he anticipated and set the framework of discussion for most major theological issues of our day. This presentation was designed to show why Buber has strenuously opposed the influence of this genius to whom he is himself so much indebted.

One of the Hasidic tales may serve as a final comment on Buber's attitude toward the kind of strained Paulinism that Kierkegaard represents.

> A Hasid of the Rabbi of Lubin once fasted from one sabbath to the next. On Friday afternoon he began to suffer such cruel thirst that he thought he would die. He saw a well, went up to it, and prepared to drink. But instantly he realized that because of the one brief hour he had still to endure, he was about to destroy the work of the entire week. He did not drink and went away from the well.

> Then he was touched by a feeling of pride for having passed this difficult test. When he became aware of it, he said to himself: "Better I go and drink than let my heart fall prey to pride." He went back to the well, but just as he was going to bend down to draw water, he noticed that his thirst had disappeared.
>
> When the sabbath had begun, he entered his teacher's house. "Patchwork!" the Rabbi called to him as he entered the threshold.[61]

We have noted that Buber's reading of the Pauline literature is one-sided; we must now note a similar limitation in his view of the Pauline influence. Kierkegaard's is not the only possible Christian response to this literature. Reinhold Niebuhr, one of the most influential interpreters of Paul in our time, has produced a socially-oriented Paulinism which is inexplicable in terms of Buber's analysis of the Pauline message. Far from using it as an instrument for anguished soul-searching on the part of the isolated individual who withdraws from the "world," Niebuhr has fashioned his Pauline outlook into an instrument of brilliant historical analysis and into a springboard from which he has carried on an unceasing fight for social justice. Furthermore, in doing so, Niebuhr echoes the emphasis of a major Protestant tradition, the Calvinist, which has often combined Pauline theology with a profound concern for the social order.[62]

Some commentators insist that Niebuhr's political activities and social concerns have been manifested independently of, or in outright opposition to, his Pauline theology. This is generally the view of those who know a good bit about social science or some other discipline but nothing about religion, or at least nothing beyond the clichés absorbed in the course of youthful training in some other area. Niebuhr's religious and social thought is all of a piece, but his reading of Paul is as selective as is Buber's reading of Hasidism, and for the same reason; he is not concerned with presenting a balanced account of a body of literature. He responds to, and, in part, reshapes an outlook to which he has himself been converted in order to fashion an existentially relevant understanding of the relation between God and man.

In the Pauline view of sin Niebuhr finds the search for a basis upon which human freedom and the depth of man's involvement in sin may be simultaneously affirmed. He does not find a fatalistic account of how men became enslaved to sin through their implication in the fall of Adam. "Original sin," the term used to convey this insight, is itself paradoxical.

> The Christian doctrine of original sin with its seemingly contradictory assertions about the inevitability of sin and man's responsibility for sin is a dialectical truth which does justice to the fact that man's self-love and self-centeredness is inevitable, but not in such a way as to fit into the category of natural necessity. It is within and by his freedom that man sins. The final paradox is that the discovery of the inevitability of sin is man's highest assertion of freedom.[63]

As Niebuhr expresses it here, the doctrine of original sin is a total understanding of man amidst the drama of history; it is not the result of apocalyptic plumbing of the hidden depths of the divine plan. Its practical significance is that man's recognition of the inevitability of his self-centeredness chastens his pride. If he comes to realize the depths of his self-absorption, he may struggle against the injustice, the self-interested action, that is its social expression.

Niebuhr's Paulinism leads him to a moral position that is marked by tremendous tension. The cross serves as a symbol of the suffering love of Jesus, whose perfection the Christian is to emulate. Since man always falls short of Jesus' example, the cross also symbolizes the forgiveness of God as mediated by Jesus Christ. But this tension between the moral and religious dimensions, between man's effortful failure and God's gracious forgiveness, does not lead Niebuhr to the kind of despair and withdrawal that Buber regards as the inevitable fruit of Pauline thinking. The element of moral activism is introduced by the fact that the forgiveness of God mediated by the cross does not release men from the obligation of trying to express perfect love.* And the expression of love in the corporate dimension of life, where the numbers involved make personal relations impossible, is, in Niebuhr's view, the prophetic passion for social justice.

As the Pharisees rejected Jesus' version of the absolute character of the divine demand, so Buber, true to the spirit of Judaism, rejects the notion that men ought to be judged by the standard of the perfect love expressed from the cross, or by any other perfect standard: "For our God makes only one demand upon us. He does not expect a humanly unattainable completeness and perfection, but only the willingness to do as much as we possibly can at every single instant." [64] This is a significant difference that makes Buber's thought less anguished than Niebuhr's, but Niebuhr's socially ori-

* Compare the Rabbinic teaching: "It is not thy part to finish the task, yet thou art not free to desist from it." (Aboth 2:16)

ented Paulinism still stands as a striking, and by no means trivial, exception to Buber's portrait of the debilitating influence of Pauline thought.

Niebuhr is a particularly felicitous thinker to compare with Buber, because their thinking is similar in many ways; so that a further examination of the differences between them will enable us to appreciate the Jewish character of Buber's existentialism. They both adopt an existential approach to truth which owes much to the perspectives of the Hebrew Bible (Niebuhr has achieved a remarkable fusion — fusion, not an artificial juxtaposition — of prophetic and Pauline insights), but their thought displays a strikingly different tone, which is largely attributable to differences between Judaism and Christianity.

Niebuhr's pessimism regarding man's capacity to fulfill the divine demand leads him to posit his own version of justification by faith. Men are generally self-centered but they are sometimes drawn out of themselves by the force of circumstances — from the standpoint of faith, this is to be understood as the grace of God — and their response is one of love. This is not unlike Buber's view of the combination of spontaneity and decision, the "being chosen and choosing," that stands at the heart of the I-Thou encounter. But where Buber emphasizes the active element, the stepping into relation ("We have to be concerned . . . not about grace but about will"), Niebuhr emphasizes the power beyond the self, the divine grace, that draws the self out of its anxious self-preoccupation. He does so because he sees no greater source of evil than the self-congratulatory attitude of a man who has just achieved some measure of virtue. It is important for the righteous to realize that they are justified by faith, by the empowering grace of God, in order that their inclination to self-righteousness may be tempered by humility.

There are two great moral evils that afflict the majority of men who, like Buber's sinners, are not radically evil but slip into it time and again. One is passivity in the face of injustice; the other is self-righteousness at moral achievement. Buber, true to the tendency of Judaism, has concentrated the full power of his rhetoric against the first; Niebuhr, true to the tendency of Christianity, has exerted his efforts against the other. Both evils are, of course, treated by these thinkers and by their respective traditions; the difference between them is one of emphasis. And the difference in emphasis will become even clearer if we pursue the comparison further.

It is typical of the somber character of Niebuhr's thought that he should regard the experience of conversion to Christian Faith — the consummation of the Christian mission — as a peril to the soul. For the convert may use the experience as an excuse for relaxing. He may lose the tension between his striving for justice and love and his recognition that the failure which is inevitably involved is one that sets him in continual need of God's forgiveness. This is a hard teaching; it chastens pride and complacency. While not certain that Paul intended his description of himself as sinner to apply after his conversion just as much as it did before that event, Niebuhr is certain that it should have been so intended. He wrote that, ". . . ages of Christian experience were required to disclose that a righteousness 'by grace' may lead to new forms of Pharisaism [here used in the New Testament sense of 'self-righteousness'] if it does not recognize that forgiveness is as necessary at the end as at the beginning of the Christian life." [65]

Buber agrees that the life of faith knows no final point at

which the individual may regard himself as having fully attained the life of virtue. We may recall his view that man must strive to unite the basic drives of life in the one true direction, to unite them by consecrating them to God. In this connection he notes that, "Just as a soul most unitary from birth is sometimes beset by inner difficulties, thus even a soul most powerfully struggling for unity can never completely achieve it." But where, if he were to use Buber's terms, Niebuhr would warn against the grave perils involved for the soul that imagines its unity, its God-centered quality, to be more complete than is actually the case, Buber is far more optimistic.

> . . . any work that I do with a united soul reacts upon my soul, acts in the direction of new and greater unification, leads me, though by all sorts of detours, to a *steadier* unity than was the preceding one. Thus man ultimately reaches a point where he can rely upon his soul, because its unity is now so great that it overcomes contradiction with effortless ease. Vigilance, of course, is necessary even then, but it is a relaxed vigilance.[66]

This statement reflects Buber's understanding of Hasidism, but we may remember that he regards Hasidism as a concentrated form of an outlook that is to be found throughout Judaism. He has noted that in the Talmud, "The play of the imagination upon the sin is explained as being even more serious than the sin itself, because it is this which alienates the soul from God." [67] It alienates the soul from God by encouraging it to preoccupation with itself when what is needed is a turning toward the other. "Original guilt," he says, "consists in remaining with oneself," [68] whereas, as he declared in another context: "All real living is meeting." [69]

Despite their differences, this comparison of the thought of Buber and Niebuhr reveals so many similarities that readers may suspect that their interpretations of their respective traditions are not authentic. This is emphatically not the case.

Abraham J. Heschel, one of the truly great Jewish scholars of our time, has written an essay on Reinhold Niebuhr in which he shows that in every age the Jewish tradition has manifested a profound awareness of the pervasiveness and intractability of human sinfulness.[70] While reading Heschel's essay we see that the Jewish understanding of man has more in common with the Paulinism of Niebuhr than it has with the facile optimism to be found in certain rationalistic presentations of Judaism. But Heschel, having shown the extent of Jewish sensitivity to sin, points to the fact that ultimately the Jewish understanding parts company with the somber view of man found in Niebuhr's thought or in any other version of Paulinism. In the final analysis, the Mitzvah, the sacred commandment, remains the focus of Jewish piety, and, paraphrasing Kant's axiom, "I ought, therefore I can," Heschel notes that a presupposition of the idea of Mitzvah is: "Thou art commanded, therefore thou canst." [71] As we have noted, Buber invariably expresses this positive attitude of the Jewish tradition toward the power of the human will, by emphasizing the fact that the turning is always possible, and he too, has a variant of this Kantian axiom. "Man can choose God," says Buber, "and he can reject God. That man may fall implies that he may rise; that man has power to lead the world to perdition implies that he has power to lead the world to redemption." [72]

Traditions such as Judaism and Christianity are far too complex to be treated as though each had only one view of man, one approach to revelation, and one theology. Many Christian thinkers and movements are extremely optimistic in their view of man, and there are extremely pessimistic thinkers and movements to be found within the Jewish tradition. Niebuhr has provided a clear statement of the character of their differences: ". . . there are differences in emphasis in both the diagnosis of the human situation and the religious assurances corresponding to the diagnosis. But there is no simple contrast." [73]

If the difference between the Jewish and Christian understanding of man is one of emphasis, at one point their differences are radical and irreconcilable. That is their attitudes toward Jesus of Nazareth. Where the Christian sees in Jesus the Incarnation, God's assumption of human form, Buber, as a Jew, sees a process of deification of the founder of a faith on the part of his followers. Furthermore, Christianity, in proclaiming Jesus as the Christ, the Messiah, declares that redemption, the fulfillment of the messianic hope, has already taken place.[74] Against this, Buber sets the basic Jewish conviction that God's redeeming power is at work everywhere and at all times but that the messianic state of redemption has not yet come.

Addressing an audience composed of Christians who were carrying on a "mission to the Jews," Buber spoke of the book and the expectation which the two faiths hold in common. The book, of course, is the Old Testament, fulfilled by the New Testament for the Christians, but for the Jews, it is *the* Bible. The expectation is the messianic one. "Your expectation," he said, "is directed toward a second coming, ours to a coming which has not been anticipated by a first." This led him to stress the unbridgeable gulf that divides the two faiths. "Pre-messianically our destinies are divided.

Now to the Christian the Jew is the incomprehensibly obdurate man, who declines to see what has happened; and to the Jew the Christian is the incomprehensibly daring man, who affirms in an unredeemed world that its redemption has been accomplished. This is a gulf which no human power can bridge."[75]

The matter does not rest there. Buber continued by pointing the way to a reconciliation between Christians and Jews in the face of this unalterable difference.

> It behooves both you and us to hold inviolably fast to our own true faith, that is to our own deepest relationship to truth. It behooves both of us to show a religious respect for the true faith of the other. This is not what is called "tolerance," our task is not to tolerate each other's waywardness but to acknowledge the real relationship in which both stand to the truth. Whenever we both, Christian and Jew, care more for God Himself than for our images of God, we are united in the feeling that our Father's house is differently constructed than our human models take it to be.[76]

This position should not be confused with the relativism of liberal theology, which holds that all great religions are valid to a certain extent. The very image that has often been used in expounding the liberal position points to the difference. Liberal thinkers speak of the divine as a statue in the middle of a clearing and of the great religions as different paths leading to it. From each path a different, but objectively valid, view of the statue is obtained. But for Buber no Thou can be known with objective validity, and this is especially true of the eternal Thou, for, ". . . it is . . . only the relation I-Thou in which we can meet God at all, because of Him, in absolute contrast to all other existing beings, no objective aspect can be attained."[77]

Each faith must be proven true in the life of the faithful. Although all of them embody meaning—meaning as encounter—none of the adherents of any faith can be certain, in the sense of *objective* validation, that their particular faith reflects even a facet of truth. Together, in holy insecurity, they make the venture of the infinite.

Epilogue: Courage

ONE day I remarked to Martin Buber that Freud is reported to have answered a question concerning the meaning of life, by saying that it is work and love. Buber laughed and said that this was good, but not complete. He would say: work, love, faith, and humor.

This sort of badinage is not likely to uncover the meaning of life, but the terms "work, love, faith, and humor" do go a long way toward describing Buber himself. Yet in this list one crucial characteristic of the man is omitted — courage; and in Buber, courage has a cast that is peculiarly Jewish.

Other religions have often retreated from the evils of nature and history by declaring that the God of creation was evil, and that some redeemer was necessary to rescue man from His work. Judaism, in the Bible, and throughout the course of its long history, has resolutely affirmed that God, Creator and Redeemer, is one; and that this one God, and the world He has created, are good. In this insistence on the goodness of the Creator and His creation some critics have seen a blinking of the tragic elements of existence on the part of Judaism. Buber objects: "What saved Judaism is not . . . the fact that it failed to experience 'the tragedy,' the contradiction in the world's process, deeply enough; but rather that it experienced that 'tragedy' in the dialogical situation, which means that it experienced *the contradiction as theophany.*" [1] Judaism came to see the evils to which it has been subjected throughout history as an appearance of God, because in the midst of encounter it could experience them as a test of its faith and a challenge to redemptive action.

Buber first wrote of the contradiction as theophany in 1928. A few years later he was a party to the greatest test to which his words could be subjected; he lived as a Jew in Hitler's Germany.

Buber stood this test by witnessing to the God of his fathers in the midst of the anguish. The words that he spoke and wrote between 1933 and 1935 show how deeply he experienced the contradiction — the evil that was rampant. He wrote with intense pain of the situation Jewish children encountered in the first years of Nazi rule. Their friends, schoolmates, and teachers suddenly changed their behavior toward them, and the symbol of this change was the shift from the friendly smile to the mocking leer.[2]

The trial was agonizing, but not shattering for Buber, because he sees trials of this kind as part of Israel's destiny. He constantly reminded his people of the resources of their Faith, he reminded them that, ". . . to Israel belongs the grace to ever renew the primordial bond [the Sinai covenant] by which it first came into being, in just such distress." [3]

He saw the need for confession of sin as the first step. In 1933, when their time of testing had begun, Buber chose the period of the High Holy Days — holidays whose liturgy (on the Day of Atonement) contains a corporate confession of sin — to remind the Jews that they must not look outward and attempt to derive some consolation by declaring that they are less sinful than the Germans. He insisted that they look inward and consider the tepid quality of Jewish existence, the greed and empty cleverness that characterized Jewish life, and that doing this, they would realize that, "No one is free of guilt, no one may exclude himself from it." [4]

Only a man with Buber's passionate involvement in the "prophetic faith" could have had the courage to urge his people to confession at a time like that; a time when most religious leaders compare the virtue of their own people to the sins of the oppressors and indulge in endless cries of self-justification or self-pity. Buber insisted that self-justification was the wrong response. He said that the Jews of Germany could neither control the Germans nor their historical situation. Therefore, he urged them to turn their attention to things they could control; he urged them to engage in confession, self-criticism, and the effort to establish genuine community among themselves. He used the analogy of a farmer in the time of drought; he cannot control the weather, but this is no reason for him to stop looking after his fields. He must tend them carefully and leave the weather to God so that, should the rain come, the fields will be ready.[5]

Since Buber lived the Nazi persecution as a "hiding of God," he was not utterly cut off from Him. "It ceases to be a hiding," a Zaddik once said, "if you know it is a hiding." [6] Buber was, in fact, able to see the contradiction as theophany.

Years later, when addressing an audience of American Jews he spoke of the Nazi horror in terms of the book of Job. As Job, in anguish, demanded to know why he, an innocent man, suffered, so contemporary Jews must ask why six million Jews — who were so much less sinful than their Nazi oppressors — were destroyed. Buber noted that God did not answer Job's question. "The true answer that Job receives is

God's appearance only, only that distance turns into nearness, that 'his eye sees Him,' (42:5) that he knows Him again. Nothing is explained, nothing adjusted; wrong has not become right, nor cruelty kindness. Nothing has happened but that man again hears God's address." [7]

Buber then applies the message of Job to the situation facing the Jews of today.

> And we?
>
> We — by that is meant all those who have not got over what happened and who will not get over it. How is it with us? Do we stand overcome before the hidden face of God as the tragic hero of the Greeks before faceless fate? No, rather even now we contend, we too, with God, even with Him, the Lord of Being, whom we once, we here, chose for our Lord. We do not put up with earthly being, we struggle for its redemption, and struggling we appeal to the help of our Lord, who is again and still a hiding one.
>
> In such a state we await His voice, whether it come out of the storm or out of a stillness which follows it. Though His coming appearance resemble no earlier one, we shall recognize again our cruel and merciful Lord.[8]

The sense in which Martin Buber has not only spoken these words of courage but has lived them, may best be conveyed by an incident that occurred after his first public address in America. His talk on "Judaism and Civilization" was critical of the failure of the political policies of the State of Israel to serve the ideal of Zion.[9] At its end, there was a question period, and one of his listeners asked, "If, as you say, Israel has so far been nothing more than another political state in the Near East, this is, after all, not such a terrible thing, why does it cause you to despair?" Buber leaned toward the audience searching for his interlocutor:

> Despair! Despair!? In the darkest days of our history I did not despair and I certainly do not despair now! [10]

Notes

MARTIN BUBER'S WRITINGS have been translated into English by various scholars under the auspices of a number of different publishing houses. For this reason, they lack uniformity in the transliteration of Hebrew terms, in the capitalization of technical terms, and in the capitalization of pronouns referring to God. To achieve a greater degree of clarity in the presentation of Buber's thought to an English audience, I have taken the liberty of bringing direct quotations from the English translations of his work into conformity with my own practices.

In transliterating Hebrew words I have chosen those usages that would make their pronunciation as accessible as possible to readers who are not familiar with the technical phonetic system. Technical terms derived from the Hebrew such as "Hasidic" and "Kabbalah" are capitalized. I vary from some of Buber's translators in not capitalizing such terms as "existentialism" and "absolute," and in capitalizing the third person pronoun when it refers to God.

Biblical verses included in direct quotations from the writings of Martin Buber are given as he renders them. Other quotations from the Old Testament are taken from the 1917 translation by Jewish Scholars published by the Jewish Publication Society, Philadelphia, and by George Routledge and Sons, London. New Testament quotations (except where otherwise specified) are from the King James Version.

Buber's move to Israel in 1938 led him to begin writing in Hebrew. Since that date, some of his work has appeared in Hebrew, some in German, and some in both Hebrew and German versions. The language from which Buber's translators have worked is given in the notes which follow.

Chapter 1

1. Hans Kohn, *Martin Buber: Sein Werk und seine Zeit, Ein Versuch über Religion und Politik* (Hellerau: Verlag Jacob Hegner, 1930).
2. Ibid. as quoted on p. 29. (my translation)

3. Martin Buber, *Hasidism and Modern Man,* trans. from the German and ed. by Maurice S. Friedman (New York: Horizon Press, 1958), "My Way to Hasidism," pp. 55ff.
4. Ibid. p. 58.
5. Martin Buber, *The Prophetic Faith,* trans. from the Hebrew by Carlyle Witton-Davies (New York: The Macmillan Co., 1949), p. 46.
6. Martin Buber, *I and Thou,* trans. from the German by Ronald Gregor Smith (Edinburgh: T. & T. Clark, 1937). A "Postscript" by the author has now appeared (2nd ed., New York: Charles Scribner's Sons, 1958). Original German edition, *Ich und Du* (Leipzig: Insel Verlag, 1923).
7. See Ernest M. Wolf, "Martin Buber and German Jewry," *Judaism* (Oct. 1952), pp. 351f.
8. Martin Buber, *Paths in Utopia,* trans. from the German by R. F. C. Hull (New York: The Macmillan Co., 1950).
9. Martin Buber, *Israel and Palestine, The History of an Idea,* trans. from the German by Stanley Godman (London: East and West Library, 1952).

Chapter 2

1. Martin Buber, *Tales of the Hasidim, The Later Masters,* trans. from the German by Olga Marx (New York: Schocken Books, 1948), "Master and Disciple," p. 261.
2. For excellent discussions of existentialism see: David E. Roberts, *Existentialism and Religious Belief,* ed. by Roger Hazelton (New York: Oxford University Press, 1957) and William Barrett, *Irrational Man* (New York: Doubleday & Co., 1958).
3. "Being-toward-one's-death" is an attempt to render "das-Sein-zum-Tod," a central category from Martin Heidegger's *Sein und Zeit* (6th ed., Tübingen: Neomarius Verlag, 1949).
4. Marjorie Grene, *Dreadful Freedom: A Critique of Existentialism* (Chicago: University of Chicago Press, 1948). See also Helmut Kuhn, *Encounter with Nothingness: An Essay on Existentialism* (Chicago: Henry Regnery, 1949) and Norberto Bobbio, *The Philosophy of Decadentism: A Study in Existentialism,* trans. from the Italian by David Moore (Oxford: Basil Blackwell, 1948).
5. Maurice S. Friedman, *Martin Buber: The Life of Dialogue* (Chicago: University of Chicago Press, 1955), p. 27; Arthur A. Cohen,

Martin Buber (New York: Hillary House, 1957), p. 33; *The Writings of Martin Buber*, ed. by Will Herberg (New York: Meridian Books, 1956), see "Editor's Introduction," pp. 12f.

6. *I and Thou*, p. 3.
7. William G. Cole, *Sex in Christianity and Psychoanalysis* (New York: Oxford University Press, 1955), p. 26.
8. *I and Thou*, p. 65.
9. Ibid. pp. 114f.
10. Ibid. pp. 67f.
11. Martin Buber, *Eclipse of God, Studies in the Relation Between Religion and Philosophy* (New York: Harper & Brothers, 1952), "God and the Spirit of Man," trans. from the German by Maurice S. Friedman, p. 163.
12. *I and Thou*, p. 34.
13. Jacob B. Agus, *Modern Philosophies of Judaism* (New York: Behrman's Jewish Book House, 1941), pp. 239ff.
14. *I and Thou*, p. 11.
15. Ibid.
16. Ibid. p. 78.
17. Ibid. p. 33.
18. Ibid.
19. Ibid. p. 9.
20. Ibid. p. 3.
21. Ibid. p. 33.
22. Ibid. p. 17.
23. Ibid. p. 16.
24. Ibid. p. 15.
25. Ibid. pp. 98f.
26. Ibid. pp. 14f.
27. Ibid. p. 16.
28. Martin Buber, *Between Man and Man*, trans. from the German by Ronald Gregor Smith (London: Routledge & Kegan Paul, 1947), "Dialogue," p. 35.
29. Ibid.
30. *I and Thou*, p. 98.
31. Ibid. p. 7.
32. Ibid. p. 8.
33. Ibid.
34. Ibid. p. 9.
35. Ibid. "Postscript," pp. 131–4.
36. Ibid. "Postscript," p. 126.

37. Ibid. "Postscript," pp. 124–30.
38. Ibid. p. 31.
39. Agus, op. cit. p. 276.
40. Martin Buber, *Israel and the World, Essays in a Time of Crisis* (New York: Schocken Books, 1948), "The Prejudices of Youth," trans. from the German by Olga Marx, p. 46. See also *Between Man and Man*, "The Education of Character," pp. 108ff., 116f.
41. Ibid. "What Is Man?", p. 184.
42. Ibid. "The Question to the Single One," p. 71.
43. *I and Thou*, p. 7.
44. Ibid. pp. 41f.
45. *Eclipse of God*, "Religion and Philosophy," trans. from the German by Maurice S. Friedman, p. 50.
46. *Between Man and Man*, "Dialogue," p. 25.
47. *Eclipse of God*, "Religion and Philosophy," p. 49.
48. Martin Buber, *Pointing the Way*, trans. from the German and ed. by Maurice S. Friedman (New York: Harper & Brothers, 1957), "Bergson's Concept of Intuition," p. 84.
49. Ibid.

Chapter 3

1. *I and Thou*, p. 6. See also p. 75.
2. Ibid. p. 80.
3. Ibid. p. 78.
4. Ibid. p. 101.
5. Ibid. pp. 80f.
6. Martin Buber, *Tales of the Hasidim, The Early Masters*, trans. from the German by Olga Marx (New York: Schocken Books, 1947), "Question and Answer," p. 269.
7. *Between Man and Man*, "Dialogue," p. 15.
8. *Eclipse of God*, "Religion and Philosophy," p. 62.
9. Ibid. p. 56.
10. Ibid. p. 43.
11. *Between Man and Man*, "The Question to the Single One," p. 57.
12. Martin Buber, *Hasidism* (New York: Philosophical Library, 1948), "Spinoza, Sabbatai Zevi, and the Baalshem," trans. from the German by Greta Hort and revised with the help of Carlyle Witton-Davies, p. 97.
13. *I and Thou*, "Postscript," p. 135.

14. *Eclipse of God*, "Religion and Reality," trans. from the German by Norbert Guterman, p. 25.
15. Ibid. "The Love of God and the Idea of Deity," trans. from the Hebrew by I. M. Lask, p. 84. Also included in *Israel and the World*, p. 65.
16. *I and Thou*, p. 77.
17. *Eclipse of God*, "Religion and Ethics," trans. from the German by Eugene Kamenka and Maurice S. Friedman, p. 127.
18. Ibid. "Religion and Philosophy," pp. 62f.
19. *Israel and the World*, "The Faith of Judaism," trans. from the German by Greta Hort, p. 17.
20. Loc. cit. p. 25.
21. *Eclipse of God*, "Religion and Philosophy," pp. 59f.
22. Ibid. "Religion and Ethics," p. 129.
23. *Israel and the World*, "The Faith of Judaism," p. 15. See also *Tales of the Hasidim, The Early Masters*, "The Song of You," p. 212.
24. *I and Thou*, p. 79.
25. *Eclipse of God*, "The Love of God and the Idea of Deity," p. 81; *Israel and the World*, p. 63.
26. *I and Thou*, pp. 87f.
27. Ibid. p. 87.
28. *Eclipse of God*, "Prelude: Report on Two Talks," trans. from the German by Maurice S. Friedman, pp. 17f. See also *I and Thou*, pp. 75f.
29. *Eclipse of God*, "Prelude: Report on Two Talks," p. 18.
30. Arthur A. Cohen, "Book Review of *Eclipse of God* by Martin Buber," *Judaism* (July 1953), pp. 282f.
31. Martin Buber, *For the Sake of Heaven*, trans. from the German by Ludwig Lewisohn (2nd ed., New York: Meridian Books; and Philadelphia: The Jewish Publication Society of America, 1958), "Author's Foreword to the New Edition," p. xiii.
32. *I and Thou*, p. 118.
33. *Eclipse of God*, "Reply to C. G. Jung," trans. from the German by Maurice S. Friedman, pp. 173f.
34. Martin Buber, *Dialogisches Leben* (Zürich: Gregor Müller Verlag, 1947), "Die Frage an den Einzelnen," p. 197 (my translation). Appears in *Between Man and Man*, "The Question to the Single One," p. 45.
35. *Eclipse of God*, "God and the Spirit of Man," pp. 166f. See also ibid. "Religion and Philosophy," p. 40, "Religion and Modern

Thinking," trans. from the German by Maurice S. Friedman, p. 93, "God and the Spirit of Man," p. 160; *I and Thou*, pp. 47ff.; *Paths in Utopia*, ch. X; *Israel and the World*, "The Prejudices of Youth," pp. 50f.

36. *Pointing the Way*, "Education and World View," p. 104.
37. *I and Thou*, pp. 104ff.
38. *Pointing the Way*, "Education and World View," p. 104.
39. Ibid. "Genuine Dialogue and the Possibilities of Peace," p. 238.
40. *I and Thou*, p. 106.
41. *Eclipse of God*, "Religion and Modern Thinking," p. 93.
42. *I and Thou*, pp. 116f.
43. Ibid. pp. 110f.
44. *Eclipse of God*, "Religion and Philosophy," p. 50.
45. Paul Tillich, *Systematic Theology*, vol. I (Chicago: University of Chicago Press, 1951–), p. 126.
46. *Eclipse of God*, "Religion and Philosophy," p. 50.
47. Ibid. "Religion and Modern Thinking," p. 89. See also ibid. p. 101, "Religion and Ethics," p. 139; *The Prophetic Faith*, pp. 44, 177, 193; Martin Buber, *At the Turning* (New York: Farrar, Straus and Young, 1952), "The Dialogue Between Heaven and Earth," pp. 58ff.; Martin Buber, *Two Types of Faith*, trans. from the German by Norman P. Goldhawk (New York: The Macmillan Co., 1951), pp. 129ff.
48. *Between Man and Man*, "Dialogue," p. 11.
49. *I and Thou*, "Postscript," p. 137.
50. *Between Man and Man*, "The Education of Character," p. 117.
51. *I and Thou*, p. 112. See also ibid. pp. 75, 100.
52. Ibid. p. 112.
53. *Eclipse of God*, "Religion and Reality," p. 34. See also ibid. "Religion and Modern Thinking," pp. 89ff., and "God and the Spirit of Man," pp. 164ff.
54. *I and Thou*, p. 11. Also cited on pp. 25 and 47 of this work.
55. *Eclipse of God*, "Religion and Modern Thinking," p. 91.
56. *The Prophetic Faith*, p. 177.
57. Basil Mitchell, contribution to "The *University* Discussion," of "Theology and Falsification," in *New Essays in Philosophical Theology*, Antony Flew and Alasdair MacIntyre, eds. (New York: The Macmillan Co., 1955), pp. 103–5.
58. *At the Turning*, "The Dialogue Between Heaven and Earth," pp. 47ff.
59. *Hasidism*, "Spinoza, Sabbatai Zevi, and the Baalshem," p. 96.

Chapter 4

1. Martin Buber and Franz Rosenzweig, *Die Schrift und ihre Verdeutschung* (Berlin: Schocken Verlag, 1936), "Der Mensch von heute und die judische Bibel," p. 45.
2. This quotation is taken from a letter from Martin Buber to the author, dated Sept. 19, 1957.
3. See, Maurice S. Friedman, *Martin Buber: The Life of Dialogue,* p. 257; *The Writings of Martin Buber,* ed. by Will Herberg, "Editor's Introduction," pp. 24f.
4. Martin Buber, *Good and Evil* (New York: Charles Scribner's Sons, 1953), "Right and Wrong," trans. from the German by Ronald Gregor Smith, p. 56.
5. Solomon Schechter, *Seminary Addresses and Other Papers* (Cincinnati: Ark Publishing Co., 1915), "Higher Criticism Higher Anti-Semitism."
6. *The Prophetic Faith,* pp. 45f.
7. Martin Buber, *Moses,* trans. from the Hebrew by I. M. Lask (Oxford and London: East and West Library, 1946), pp. 157f.
8. *The Prophetic Faith,* pp. 108ff.
9. Martin Buber, "Abraham the Seer," trans. from the German by Sophie Meyer, *Judaism* (Fall 1956), pp. 291f.
10. Ibid. p. 293.
11. *Moses,* pp. 6f. See also *The Prophetic Faith,* p. 4.
12. Ibid. p. 94.
13. Martin Buber, "Genesisprobleme," *Monatsschrift für Geschichte und Wissenschaft des Judentums* (1936), pp. 84f.
14. *The Prophetic Faith,* p. 6. See also *Moses,* p. 158.
15. Ibid. pp. 119–24, 130–36.
16. H. L. Ginzberg, "New Trends in Biblical Criticism," *Commentary* (Sept. 1950), pp. 276–84.
17. H. Richard Niebuhr, *The Meaning of Revelation* (New York: The Macmillan Co., 1946), pp. 60f.
18. Ibid. pp. 61ff.
19. *Moses,* p. 18.
20. Ibid. p. 16.
21. Ibid.
22. Ibid. p. 75.
23. Ibid. p. 17.

24. *Israel and the World,* "The Man of Today and the Jewish Bible," trans. from the German by Olga Marx, p. 97.
25. *Moses,* p. 75.
26. *Tales of the Hasidim, The Early Masters,* "The Famous Miracle," p. 71.
27. *Moses,* p. 77.
28. Ibid. p. 17.
29. *At the Turning,* "The Dialogue Between Heaven and Earth," p. 49. (my emphasis)
30. Martin Buber, *The Legend of the Baal-Shem,* trans. from the German by Maurice S. Friedman (New York: Harper & Brothers, 1955), "The Life of the Hasidim," p. 41. See also Martin Buber, *Die Schrift und ihre Verdeutschung,* "Über die Wortwahl in einer Verdeutschung der Schrift," p. 138.
31. *Eclipse of God,* "Supplement: Reply to C. G. Jung," p. 173.
32. *The Prophetic Faith,* p. 164. See also *Hasidism,* "Symbolical and Sacramental Existence in Judaism," trans. from the German by Greta Hort and revised with the help of Carlyle Witton-Davies, p. 121.
33. *I and Thou,* p. 117.
34. Ibid.
35. Loc. cit. p. 64.
36. *Hasidism,* "Symbolical and Sacramental Existence in Judaism," p. 142.
37. *Israel and the World,* "False Prophets," trans. from the German by Olga Marx, pp. 113–18. See also *The Prophetic Faith,* pp. 176–80.
38. Ibid. pp. 176f.
39. Loc. cit. pp. 58, 80.
40. *Israel and the World,* "The Man of Today and the Jewish Bible," p. 94.
41. Soren Kierkegaard, *Philosophical Fragments or a Fragment of Philosophy,* trans. with introduction and notes by David F. Swenson (Princeton: Princeton University Press, 1946), pp. 47–51, 74–88.
42. *The Passover Haggadah,* trans. from the Hebrew and Aramaic by Rabbi Albert S. Goldstein (New York: National Jewish Welfare Board, 1952), p. 53.
43. *Israel and the World,* "Why We Should Study Jewish Sources," trans. from the German by Olga Marx, p. 146.
44. Ibid. "Teaching and Deed," trans. from the German by Olga Marx, p. 139.

45. *Tales of the Hasidim, The Later Masters,* "In His Father's Footsteps," p. 157.
46. Ibid. "Into the Word," p. 169.
47. *Between Man and Man,* "Dialogue," p. 7.
48. *Eclipse of God,* "The Love of God and the Idea of Deity," pp. 81f., *Israel and the World,* p. 63.
49. Ibid. "What Are We To Do about the Ten Commandments?", trans. from the German by Olga Marx, p. 85.
50. "Abraham the Seer," *Judaism* (Fall 1956), pp. 293ff.
51. Ibid. p. 295.
52. *At the Turning,* "Judaism and Civilization," pp. 17f.
53. *Moses,* pp. 101ff., 106ff., 115, 125ff., 186.
54. *The Prophetic Faith,* p. 66.
55. Ibid. pp. 70–154.
56. *At the Turning,* "Judaism and Civilization," p. 16.
57. *The Prophetic Faith,* pp. 83, 152f. *Moses,* p. 63.
58. *Israel and the World,* "Biblical Leadership," trans. from the German by Greta Hort, p. 130.
59. *The Prophetic Faith,* p. 2.
60. Ibid. pp. 144, 152f.
61. Ibid. pp. 215f.
62. Ibid. pp. 202ff.
63. Ibid. pp. 205f.
64. Ibid. pp. 233ff.
65. *The Two Types of Faith,* p. 110.
66. *The Prophetic Faith,* pp. 219–29.
67. Ibid. pp. 229f.
68. Ibid. p. 230.
69. *Hasidism,* "Spinoza, Sabbatai Zevi, and the Baalshem," pp. 112ff.
70. *Two Types of Faith,* p. 107.
71. Ibid. pp. 111f.
72. *Pointing the Way,* "Prophecy, Apocalyptic, and the Historical Hour," p. 200.
73. *Israel and the World,* "The Two Foci of the Jewish Soul," trans. from the German by Greta Hort, p. 37. See also *Pointing the Way,* "Prophecy, Apocalyptic, and the Historical Hour," pp. 192ff.
74. Ibid. p. 201.
75. *Two Types of Faith,* pp. 111f.
76. *At the Turning,* "Judaism and Civilization," pp. 20ff.
77. *Hasidism,* "Spinoza, Sabbatai Zevi, and the Baalshem," p. 116.

Chapter 5

1. *Hasidism,* "The Foundation Stone," trans. from the Hebrew by Carlyle and Mary Witton-Davies, pp. 43f. See also *Hasidism and Modern Man,* "My Way to Hasidism," p. 59.
2. Ibid. pp. 47–69.
3. Ibid. "Hasidism and Modern Man," pp. 21–7.
4. Gershom G. Scholem, *Major Trends in Jewish Mysticism* (New York: Schocken Books, 1946), Ninth Lecture; J. G. Weiss, "Contemplative Mysticism and 'Faith' in Hasidic Piety," *The Journal of Jewish Studies,* vol. IV, no. 1, 1953; Ernst Simon, "Martin Buber and the Faith of Israel, *Iyyun, Hebrew Philosophical Quarterly,* vol. IX, no. 1, 1958, pp. 23ff.
5. *Hasidism,* "Spirit and Body of the Hasidic Movement," trans. from the German by Greta Hort and revised with the help of Carlyle Witton-Davies, pp. 1ff., 26ff., "The Foundation Stone," pp. 34ff. See also *Israel and the World,* "The Faith of Judaism," p. 13.
6. *Two Types of Faith,* p. 77.
7. Scholem, op. cit. Eighth Lecture.
8. *Tales of the Hasidim, The Early Masters* (cited for the balance of this chapter as *The Early Masters*), p. 3.
9. Scholem, op. cit. Seventh Lecture.
10. *Hasidism,* "Spirit and Body of the Hasidic Movement," pp. 71f. See also ibid. "The Foundation Stone," pp. 55f.; *Hasidism and Modern Man,* "Hasidism and Modern Man," pp. 32f.
11. *Tales of the Hasidim, The Later Masters* (cited for the balance of this chapter as *The Later Masters*), "The Ladder," p. 170.
12. *Hasidism,* "Love of God and Love of One's Neighbor," trans. from the Hebrew by Immanuel Olsvanger and revised with the help of Carlyle Witton-Davies, p. 171. Also included in *Hasidism and Modern Man,* where it has been translated by Maurice S. Friedman from a German version of the essay, pp. 240f.
13. *Hasidism,* "Love of God and the Love of One's Neighbor," p. 168; *Hasidism and Modern Man,* p. 237.
14. *The Later Masters,* "Where To Find God," p. 235.
15. *Two Types of Faith,* p. 69.
16. Ibid. pp. 56f.
17. *Hasidism,* "The Foundation Stone," pp. 34f.

18. *The Early Masters,* "The Busy Man's Prayer," p. 69.
19. *Two Types of Faith,* p. 58.
20. *The Later Masters,* "No Graven Image," p. 279. (my emphasis)
21. *Two Types of Faith,* pp. 92ff.
22. *The Early Masters,* "Studying," pp. 286f.
23. *The Later Masters,* "Not What Goes in at the Mouth . . .", p. 229.
24. *The Later Masters,* "Against Pious Thoughts," pp. 180f.
25. Ibid. "The Fight," p. 317.
26. *The Early Masters,* "In Many Ways," p. 313.
27. *Hasidism,* "Spirit and Body of the Hasidic Movement," p. 73.
28. *The Later Masters,* "The Delay," p. 87.
29. *Hasidism,* "The Beginnings of Hasidism," pp. 17ff; *Hasidism and Modern Man,* "My Way to Hasidism," pp. 63–9.
30. *The Early Masters,* "Out of Travail," p. 280.
31. *I and Thou,* p. 3.
32. Loc. cit. p. 89.
33. *The Early Masters,* p. 4.
34. *The Later Masters,* "Each His Own," p. 147.
35. *The Early Masters,* "The Query of Queries," p. 251.
36. Loc. cit. p. 110.
37. *The Early Masters,* pp. v, vi.
38. *The Later Masters,* "His Bad Foot," p. 208.
39. Ibid. "Everywhere," p. 170.
40. Martin Buber, *Ten Rungs, Hasidic Sayings,* trans. from the German by Olga Marx (New York: Schocken Books, 1947), "Joyless Virtue," p. 44.
41. *The Later Masters,* "Most Important," p. 173.
42. *Ten Rungs, Hasidic Sayings,* "To Say Torah and Be Torah," p. 66.
43. *The Early Masters,* "To Say Torah and to Be Torah," p. 107.
44. *Hasidism and Modern Man,* "Hasidism and Modern Man," pp. 28ff.
45. *Israel and the World,* "Two Foci of the Jewish Soul," p. 34.
46. *The Later Masters,* "To the Children of Men," p. 317.
47. *At the Turning,* "The Silent Question," p. 44.

Chapter 6

1. *Eclipse of God,* "Religion and Philosophy," p. 48.
2. *Hasidism and Modern Man,* "Hasidism and Modern Man," pp. 38ff.; *Israel and the World,* "The Faith of Judaism," pp. 25ff.

3. Martin Buber, *Drei Reden über das Judentum* (Frankfurt am Main: Rütten & Loening, 1911), included in *Reden über das Judentum* (Frankfurt am Main: Rütten & Loening, 1923), reissued (Berlin: Schocken Verlag, 1932).
4. *Israel and the World*, "The Faith of Judaism," p. 13, "The Man of Today and the Jewish Bible," pp. 89ff.
5. *Good and Evil*, "Images of Good and Evil," trans. from the German by Michael Bullock, pp. 94f.
6. Ibid. p. 95.
7. Ibid. p. 97.
8. *Israel and the World*, "The Two Foci of the Jewish Soul," p. 34.
9. *Good and Evil*, "Images of Good and Evil," p. 125.
10. Ibid. p. 129.
11. Ibid. p. 130.
12. *Two Types of Faith*, pp. 83ff.
13. *Good and Evil*, "Images of Good and Evil," pp. 139f.
14. *Good and Evil*, "Right and Wrong," p. 60.
15. Maurice Friedman, *Martin Buber: The Life of Dialogue*, pp. 109ff., also a letter from Martin Buber to the author dated July 15, 1959.
16. *Pointing the Way*, "Genuine Dialogue and the Possibilities of Peace," pp. 232f.
17. Ibid. p. 233.
18. Ibid.
19. Ibid. p. 232.
20. *Two Types of Faith*, pp. 63ff., 91ff., 155ff.; *At the Turning*, "The Dialogue Between Heaven and Earth," pp. 53ff.; *Israel and the World*, "The Faith of Judaism," pp. 19ff., "The Two Foci of the Jewish Soul," pp. 32ff.
21. *Two Types of Faith*, pp. 156ff.
22. *Tales of the Hasidim, The Early Masters*, "With the Sinners," pp. 71f.
23. Talmud, *Berakhot* 34b, as quoted by Buber in *Israel and the World*, "The Faith of Judaism," p. 20. See also *Hasidism*, "The Foundation Stone," pp. 53f.
24. *Tales of the Hasidim, The Early Masters*, "Eternal Beginnings," pp. 218f.
25. *I and Thou*, p. 3. See also *Hasidism*, "The Foundation Stone," pp. 56ff.; *Israel and the World*, "The Two Foci of the Jewish Soul," pp. 33f.
26. *Drei Reden über das Judentum*, pp. 70ff.
27. *Hasidism*, "The Beginnings of Hasidism," pp. 2f.

28. *Israel and the World*, "On National Education," p. 159. See also ibid. "The Spirit of Israel and the World of Today," trans. from the Hebrew by I. M. Lask, p. 187.
29. Ibid. "The Land and Its Possessors," pp. 228f. This is an excerpt from Martin Buber, "An Open Letter to Gandhi," which appeared in Martin Buber and Judah Magnes, *Two Letters to Gandhi* (Jerusalem: Pamphlets of The Bond, Rueben Mass, 1939). A somewhat different excerpt from "An Open Letter to Gandhi," is to be found in *Pointing the Way*, "A Letter to Gandhi," in which see pp. 142f.
30. *Israel and the World*, "The Land and Its Possessors," p. 229.
31. Ibid. pp. 229f.
32. Ibid. p. 233; *Israel and Palestine*, pp. 10ff.
33. See also Exod (19:5).
34. *Israel and Palestine*, p. xi.
35. Ibid. p. 142.
36. *Pointing the Way*, "A Letter to Gandhi," pp. 143ff.; *Israel and the World*, "The Land and Its Possessors," pp. 230ff.
37. Ibid. p. 233.
38. *Israel and Palestine*, p. vii.
39. *Israel and the World*, "The Jew in the World," trans. from the German by Olga Marx, pp. 169ff., "Nationalism," trans. from the German by Olga Marx, p. 225.
40. Ibid. "The Spirit of Israel and the World of Today," p. 189. See also *Israel and Palestine*, pp. 242ff.
41. See Ernst Simon, "Martin Buber: His Way Between Thought and Deed" (on his 70th anniversary), *Jewish Frontier*, XV (Feb. 1948), p. 28.
42. *Israel and the World*, "Nationalism," p. 216.
43. *Israel and the World*, "The Land and Its Possessors," pp. 231ff.
44. Biblical verse quoted from Revised Standard Version for greater accuracy.
45. *Pointing the Way*, "A Letter to Gandhi," p. 146.
46. *Israel and the World*, "Hebrew Humanism," trans. from the German by Olga Marx, p. 246.
47. Ibid. p. 247.
48. *Israel and the World*, "And If Not Now, When?" trans. from the German by Olga Marx, p. 238.
49. *Israel and the World*, "Hebrew Humanism," p. 248.
50. *Israel and the World*, "On National Education," pp. 160f.
51. *Paths in Utopia*, ch. X; *Pointing the Way*, Section 3: Politics, Community, and Peace.

52. *Paths in Utopia*, pp. 104, 136f.; *Pointing the Way*, "Society and the State," pp. 172ff.; *Between Man and Man*, "What Is Man?", pp. 157ff.
53. *Paths in Utopia*, p. 142.
54. Ibid. p. 145.
55. Ibid. pp. 145ff.
56. Ibid. pp. 148f.
57. *Israel and Palestine*, p. 136. See also *Israel and the World*, "The Spirit of Israel and the World of Today," p. 186.
58. *The Prophetic Faith*, p. 46. Previously cited, pp. 3, 63f.
59. Martin Buber, *Kampf um Israel, Reden und Schriften* (1921–1932), (Berlin: Schocken Verlag, 1933), "Zion und die Gola," pp. 248–51.
60. *Israel and the World*, "On National Education," p. 159, "The Spirit of Israel and the World of Today," p. 187.
61. *At the Turning*, "The Silent Question," p. 42.
62. Ibid. p. 37.
63. *Hasidism*, "Spirit and Body of the Hasidic Movement," pp. 72f.
64. *Israel and the World*, "What Are We To Do about the Ten Commandments?", p. 85.
65. Ibid.
66. Ibid. p. 86.
67. Ibid. pp. 86f.
68. Ibid. p. 87.
69. Martin Buber, *Reden über das Judentum*.
70. Franz Rosenzweig, *On Jewish Learning*, ed. by Nahum N. Glatzer (New York: Schocken Books, 1955), "The Builders: Concerning the Law," pp. 72ff.
71. Ibid. pp. 77ff.
72. Ibid. pp. 83ff.
73. Ibid. pp. 86ff.
74. Franz Rosenzweig and Martin Buber, "Revelation and Law," a correspondence, trans. from the German by William Wolf and appearing as an appendix to *On Jewish Learning*, pp. 109–18.
75. Ibid. letter from Martin Buber to Franz Rosenzweig, June 24, 1924, p. 111.
76. Ibid. letters from Franz Rosenzweig to Martin Buber, June 29, 1924, p. 113, July 16, 1924, p. 116. See also ibid. "The Builders: Concerning the Law," p. 85.
77. *Iyyun, Hebrew Philosophical Quarterly*, vol. IX, no. 1, 1958 (5718). This issue includes: Ernst Simon, "Martin Buber and the

Faith of Israel," pp. 13–50; S. Hugo Bergman, "Martin Buber and Mysticism," pp. 3–12; and Nathan Rotenstreich, "Foundations of Buber's Dialogic Thinking," pp. 51–75.

78. Ibid. Ernst Simon, "Martin Buber and the Faith of Israel," pp. 14f.
79. Ibid. pp. 15ff.
80. Ibid. p. 23.
81. *On Jewish Learning,* "Revelation and Law," letter from Martin Buber to Franz Rosenzweig, June 24, 1924, p. 111.
82. *At the Turning,* "Judaism and Civilization," p. 24.
83. *Two Types of Faith,* pp. 93f.
84. Ernst Simon, "Martin Buber and the Faith of Israel," *Iyyun, Hebrew Philosophical Quarterly,* vol. IX, no. 1, 1958, pp. 18ff.
85. See Maurice Friedman, *Martin Buber, The Life of Dialogue,* ch. XXVII, "Buber and Christianity"; Paul Tillich, "Martin Buber and Christian Thought," *Commentary,* V (June 1948), pp. 515–21; Walter E. Wiest, "Martin Buber," *Ten Makers of Modern Protestant Thought,* ed. by George L. Hunt (New York: Association Press, 1958), pp. 114–26.
86. Ernst Simon, "Martin Buber: His Way Between Thought and Deed," *Jewish Frontier,* XV (Feb. 1948), p. 25.
87. *For the Sake of Heaven,* 2nd ed., "Author's Foreword to the New Edition," p. xii.

Chapter 7

1. *Two Types of Faith,* pp. 12f. See also Ernst Simon, "Martin Buber: His Way Between Thought and Deed," *Jewish Frontier,* XV (Feb. 1948), p. 26.
2. *I and Thou,* pp. 66f.
3. Ronald Gregor Smith, "The Religion of Martin Buber," *Theology Today,* vol. XII (July 1955), pp. 206–15.
4. *Between Man and Man,* "Dialogue," p. 5.
5. *Two Types of Faith,* p. 13.
6. Albert Schweitzer, *The Mystery of the Kingdom of God,* trans. with an introd. by Walter Lowrie (New York: Dodd, Mead and Co., 1914), pp. 219ff. This work has been reissued (New York: The Macmillan Co., 1950).
7. *Two Types of Faith,* pp. 106ff.
8. *Hasidism,* "Spinoza, Sabbatai Zevi, and the Baalshem," p. 114.
9. *Two Types of Faith,* pp. 24ff.
10. Ibid. p. 27.

11. Ibid. p. 28.
12. Ibid. ch. VII, pp. 56–78.
13. Ibid. pp. 56ff., 60ff.
14. Ibid. pp. 67f.
15. Ibid. pp. 68ff.
16. Ibid. p. 75.
17. Ibid. p. 115.
18. Ibid. p. 44.
19. Ibid. pp. 81f.
20. Ibid. p. 86.
21. Ibid. p. 148.
22. Ibid. pp. 81ff.
23. Ibid. p. 80.
24. Ibid. p. 141.
25. Ibid. pp. 149f.
26. Ibid. p. 89.
27. Ibid. p. 140.
28. Ibid. p. 138.
29. *Israel and the World*, "The Power of the Spirit," trans. from the German by Olga Marx, pp. 178ff.
30. Ibid. "The Spirit of Israel and the World of Today," p. 193.
31. *Two Types of Faith*, pp. 172f. See also *Eclipse of God*, "Religion and Ethics," pp. 138ff.
32. *Two Types of Faith*, pp. 7ff. See also *Eclipse of God*, "Religion and Philosophy," p. 46.
33. Ibid. pp. 9, 11f., 34.
34. Ibid. pp. 10f., 46f.
35. Ibid. pp. 30–35, 102–16, 127–34.
36. *Israel and the World*, "The God of the Nations and God," trans. from the German by Olga Marx, p. 198. See also *Two Types of Faith*, pp. 163f.
37. Ibid. pp. 10f.
38. Ibid. p. 34.
39. Ibid. p. 136.
40. Ibid. pp. 146ff.; *Eclipse of God*, "Religion and Ethics," pp. 140f.
41. *Two Types of Faith*, p. 158; *Israel and the World*, "The Two Foci of the Jewish Soul," pp. 32f.
42. *Two Types of Faith*, p. 47.
43. Ibid. pp. 52f. Buber's rendition of biblical verse is quoted.
44. Ibid. p. 80.
45. *Israel and the World*, "The Faith of Judaism," p. 18.
46. *Hasidism*, "Spirit and Body of the Hasidic Movement," p. 68; *Two Types of Faith*, p. 158; *Israel and the World*, "The Two Foci of

the Jewish Soul," pp. 32f.; *Between Man and Man*, "The Question to the Single One," p. 69.

47. *I and Thou*, p. 76.
48. *Hasidism*, "Spinoza, Sabbatai Zevi, and the Baalshem," p. 110.
49. Ibid. p. 108.
50. *Two Types of Faith*, pp. 162–9.
51. Clarence T. Craig, "Soma Christou" in *The Joy of Study*, ed. by Sherman E. Johnson (New York: The Macmillan Co., 1951), pp. 74f.; John A. T. Robinson, *The Body: A Study in Pauline Theology*, Studies in Biblical Theology, no. 5 (London: SCM Press, 1952), ch. I; Rudolf Bultmann, *Theology of the New Testament* (New York: Charles Scribner's Sons, 1951), vol. I, pp. 192–203, 232–46.
52. Martin Buber, "*The Way of Man, According to the Teachings of Hasidism*," now included in *Hasidism and Modern Man*, pp. 123–76 (no translator cited).
53. Ibid. ch. IV, pp. 153–9 and ch. V, pp. 161–7.
54. Ibid. p. 163.
55. Ibid. p. 162. See also *Tales of the Hasidim, The Later Masters*, "A Piece of Advice," p. 214.
56. Soren Kierkegaard, *Concluding Unscientific Postscript*, trans. by David F. Swenson, completed and provided with introduction and notes by Walter Lowrie (Princeton: Princeton University Press, 1944), p. 345.
57. *Between Man and Man*, "The Question to the Single One," p. 52.
58. *Eclipse of God*, "Religion and Philosophy," p. 40.
59. *Hasidism*, "Love of God and Love of One's Neighbor," p. 165; *Hasidism and Modern Man*, p. 233.
60. *I and Thou*, p. 115.
61. *Hasidism and Modern Man*, "The Way of Man," pp. 146f.; *Tales of the Hasidim, The Early Masters*, "Patchwork," p. 316.
62. John Calvin, *Institutes of the Christian Religion* (Philadelphia: Presbyterian Board of Christian Education, 1936), vol. II, Book IV, ch. XX, esp. section VIII; Ernst Troeltsch, *The Social Teachings of the Christian Churches* (London: George Allen & Unwin, Ltd., 1931), vol. II, ch. III, section 3, esp. pp. 576–92; John Dillenberger and Claude Welch, *Protestant Christianity* (New York: Charles Scribner's Sons, 1955), pp. 53–6, 99–106; John F. McNeill, *The History and Character of Calvinism* (New York: Oxford University Press, 1954), chs. XXIV and XXV.
63. Reinhold Niebuhr, *The Nature and Destiny of Man, A Christian Interpretation*, vol. I, *Human Nature*, vol. II, *Human Destiny* (New York: one-vol. ed., Charles Scribner's Sons, 1948), vol. I, p. 263.

64. *Israel and the World,* "Teaching and Deed," pp. 140f. See also *Pointing the Way,* "The Validity and Limitation of the Political Principle," p. 217; *Two Types of Faith,* p. 79; *Hasidism and Modern Man,* "Hasidism and Modern Man," pp. 31, 42.
65. Reinhold Niebuhr, op. cit. vol. II, p. 105.
66. *Hasidism and Modern Man,* "The Way of Man," p. 150.
67. *Two Types of Faith,* p. 64, cited from Joma 29.
68. *Between Man and Man,* "What Is Man?", p. 166.
69. *I and Thou,* p. 11.
70. Abraham J. Heschel, "A Hebrew Evaluation of Reinhold Niebuhr," *Reinhold Niebuhr, His Religious, Social and Political Thought,* Charles W. Kegly and Robert W. Bretall, eds., The Library of Living Theology, vol. II (New York: The Macmillan Co., 1956), pp. 393–404.
71. Ibid. p. 409.
72. *Hasidism,* "Spinoza, Sabbatai Zevi, and the Baalshem," p. 108.
73. Reinhold Niebuhr, *Pious and Secular America* (New York: Charles Scribner's Sons, 1958), "Christians and Jews in Western Civilization," p. 101.
74. *Israel and the World:* "The Two Foci of the Jewish Soul," pp. 34ff., "The Faith of Judaism," pp. 25ff., "The Spirit of Israel and the World of Today," pp. 190ff.; *Hasidism,* "Spinoza, Sabbatai Zevi, and the Baalshem," pp. 104ff.
75. *Israel and the World,* "The Two Foci of the Jewish Soul," pp. 39f.
76. Ibid. p. 40.
77. *Eclipse of God,* "God and the Spirit of Man," p. 165.

Epilogue

1. *Israel and the World,* "The Faith of Judaism," p. 26.
2. Martin Buber, *Die Stunde und die Erkenntnis, Reden und Aufsätze,* 1933–1935 (Berlin: Schocken Verlag, 1936), "Die Kinder," pp. 18ff.
3. Ibid. p. 20. (my translation)
4. Ibid. "Gericht und Erneurung," p. 25. (my translation)
5. Ibid. "Erkenntnis tut Not," pp. 59f.
6. *Tales of the Hasidim, The Early Masters,* "Hiding," p. 122.
7. *At the Turning,* "The Dialogue Between Heaven and Earth," pp. 61f.
8. Ibid. p. 62.
9. Ibid. "Judaism and Civilization," pp. 23ff.
10. I have set this incident down as I remember it.

Selected Bibliography

BOOKS BY BUBER THAT HAVE APPEARED IN ENGLISH

At the Turning, Three Addresses on Judaism. New York: Farrar, Straus and Cudahy, 1952.

Between Man and Man. New York: The Macmillan Co., 1948; London: Routledge & Kegan Paul, 1947; Paperback edition, Boston: The Beacon Press, 1955.

Eclipse of God, Studies in the Relation Between Religion and Philosophy. New York: Harper & Brothers, 1952; London: Victor Gollancz Ltd., 1953; Paperback edition, New York: Harper Torchbooks, Harper & Brothers, 1957.

For the Sake of Heaven. 2nd edition with foreword by the author, New York: Harper & Brothers, and Philadelphia: Jewish Publication Society, 1953. Paperback edition of the 2nd edition, New York: Meridian Books, Inc., and Philadelphia: The Jewish Publication Society, 1958.

Good and Evil, Two Interpretations. New York: Charles Scribner's Sons, 1953. Composed of "Right and Wrong," pp. 1–60 (see below) and "Images of Good and Evil," pp. 61–143 (see below).

Hasidism. New York: The Philosophical Library, 1948.

Hasidism and Modern Man. New York: Horizon Press, 1958.

I and Thou. 2nd edition with a "Postscript" by the author, New York: Charles Scribner's Sons, 1958; paperback edition, 1960. Original English edition, Edinburgh: T. & T. Clark, 1937.

Images of Good and Evil. London: Routledge & Kegan Paul, 1952, included in *Good and Evil* (see above).

Israel and Palestine, The History of an Idea. London: East and West Library, 1952, and issued in New York by Farrar, Straus and Cudahy.

Israel and the World, Essays in a Time of Crisis. New York: Schocken Books, 1948.

The Legend of the Baal Shem. New York: Harper & Brothers, 1955.

Mamre, Essays in Religion. London: Oxford University Press, 1946. The material in this book has reappeared, partly in *Hasidism* (see above), and partly in *Israel and the World, Essays in a Time of Crisis* (see above).

Moses. Oxford and London: East and West Library, 1946, and issued in New York by Farrar, Straus and Cudahy. Paperback edition, *Moses, The Revelation and the Covenant*. New York: Harper Torchbooks, Harper & Brothers, 1958.

Paths in Utopia. New York: The Macmillan Co., 1950; London: Routledge & Kegan Paul, 1949. Paperback edition, Boston: Beacon Press, 1959.

Pointing the Way, Collected Essays. New York: Harper & Brothers, 1957; London: Routledge & Kegan Paul, 1957.

The Prophetic Faith. New York: The Macmillan Co., 1949.

Right and Wrong, An Interpretation of Some Psalms. London: SCM Press Ltd., 1952, included in *Good and Evil* (see above).

Tales of the Hasidim, The Early Masters. New York: Schocken Books, 1947; London: Thames & Hudson, Ltd., 1955.

Tales of the Hasidim, The Later Masters. New York: Schocken Books, 1948; London: Thames & Hudson, Ltd., 1955.

The Tales of Rabbi Nachman. New York: Horizon Press, 1956.

Ten Rungs, Hasidic Sayings. New York: Schocken Books, 1947.

Two Types of Faith. New York: The Macmillan Co., 1951; London: Routledge & Kegan Paul, 1951.

The Way of Man, According to the Teachings of Hasidism. Chicago: Wilcox: Wilcox & Follet Co., 1951, included in *Hasidism and Modern Man* (see above).

Essays by Buber that Have Appeared in English but Are Not as yet Available in Book Form

"Abraham the Seer," *Judaism* (Fall 1956), pp. 291–305.

Reprint from *Psychiatry, Journal for the Study of Interpersonal Processes* (May 1957), pp. 97–129, being the Fourth Series of the William Alanson White Memorial Lectures, which include: "Distance and Relation," pp. 97–104. [This essay first appeared in *The Hibbert Journal: Quarterly Review of Religion, Theology and Philosophy* (Jan. 1951), pp. 105–13]; "Elements of the Interhuman," pp. 105–13; "Guilt and Guilt Feelings," pp. 114–29.

"Revelation and Law," a correspondence between Martin Buber and

Franz Rosenzweig which appears as an appendix to Franz Rosenzweig, *On Jewish Learning*, ed. by Nahum N. Glatzer (New York: Schocken Books, 1955), pp. 109–18.
"What Is Common to All," *The Review of Metaphysics* (March 1958), pp. 359–79.

Books in German by Martin Buber Containing Significant and as yet Untranslated Material

Daniel. Gespräche von der Verwirklichung. Leipzig: Insel Verlag, 1913.
Die Jüdische Bewegung, Gesammelte Aufsätze und Ansprachen. Vol. I, 1900–1914.; Vol. II, 1916–1920. Berlin: Jüdischer Verlag, 1916, 1921.
Kampf um Israel, Reden und Schriften (1921–1932). Berlin: Schocken Verlag, 1933.
Königtum Gottes. Vol. I, *Das Kommende Untersuchungen der Entstehungsgeschichte des Messianischen Glaubens*. Berlin: 2nd enlarged edition, Schocken Verlag, 1936.
Der Mensch und sein Gebild. Heidelberg: Verlag Lambert Schneider, 1955.
Reden über das Judentum. Collected edition. Frankfurt am Main: Rütten & Loening, 1923. Reissued under the same title, Berlin: Schocken Verlag, 1932.
Die Schrift. Translation of the Old Testament from Hebrew into German: vols. I–X, Genesis–Isaiah (in the Jewish order of the books) translated in collaboration with Franz Rosenzweig (Berlin: Verlag Lambert Schneider, from 1926); vol. XI, Jeremiah (Berlin: Verlag Lambert Schneider); vols. XII–XV, Ezekiel–Proverbs (in the Jewish order of the books) (Berlin: Schocken Verlag).
Reissued by Jacob Hegner, of Koln and Olten in three vols.: *Die Fünf Bücher der Weisung*, 1954 (the Pentateuch); *Bücher der Geschichte*, 1955 (comprised of Joshua, Judges, the two books of Samuel, and the two books of Kings); *Bücher der Kundung*, 1958 (comprised of Isaiah, Jeremiah, Ezekiel, and the book of the Twelve). The book of Psalms and the book of Proverbs have not as yet been reissued.
Martin Buber and Franz Rosenzweig, *Die Schrift und ihre Verdeutschung*. Berlin: Schocken Verlag, 1936. Contains essays by both men on the principles which guided them in their translation of the Old Testament into German.
Die Schriften über das dialogische Prinzip. Heidelberg: Verlag Lambert

Schneider, 1954. The only essay in this volume which has not appeared in English is the "Nachwort," which traces the genesis of the I-Thou, I-It distinction and Buber's relation to it.

Die Stunde und die Erkenntnis, Reden und Aufsätze, 1933–1935. Berlin: Schocken Verlag, 1936.

Worte an die Jugend. Berlin: Schocken Verlag, 1938.

Worte und die Zeit. Vol. I, *Grundsätze;* Vol. II, *Gemeinschaft.* Munich: Dreiänderverlag, 1919.

Books in English on Martin Buber

Jacob B. Agus, *Modern Philosophies of Judaism.* New York: Behrman's Jewish Book House, 1941, pp. 211–78, 376–84.

Arthur A. Cohen, *Martin Buber.* New York: Hillary House, 1957.

Maurice S. Friedman, *Martin Buber, The Life of Dialogue.* Chicago: University of Chicago Press, 1955. Paperback edition, New York: Harper Torchbooks, Harper & Brothers, 1960. Contains a full bibliography of Buber's work through that date.

Paul Schillp and Maurice S. Friedman eds., *Martin Buber.* A forthcoming volume in *The Library of Living Philosophers* series containing 24 essays on Buber by an international body of scholars, an intellectual autobiography by Buber himself, and a reply by Buber to the criticisms directed to his thought by these scholars.

English Anthologies of Martin Buber's Writings

Will Herberg ed., *The Writings of Martin Buber.* A paperback original with an introduction by the editor, pp. 1–39. New York: Meridian Books, 1956.

Jacob Trapp ed., *To Hallow This Life.* New York: Harper & Brothers, 1958 (editor's introduction, pp. ix–xiv).

Index

C